ASSAULT LANDING CRAFT

ASSAULT
DESIGN, CONSTRUCTION & OPERATIONS

LANDING CRAFT

Brian Lavery

Seaforth
P U B L I S H I N G

First published in Great Britain in 2009 by
Seaforth Publishing,
Pen & Sword Books Ltd,
47 Church Street,
Barnsley S70 2AS

www.seaforthpublishing.com

British Library Cataloguing in Publication Data
A catalogue record for this book is available from the British Library

ISBN 978 1 84832 050 5

Designed by Martin Hendry
Illustrations by Peter Wilkinson
Printed and bound in Great Britain by Cromwell Press Group, Trowbridge

PREVIOUS PAGES
*Troops landing on the
Normandy beaches from
an LCA, among much
larger landing craft.*

CONTENTS

INTRODUCTION

THE Assault Landing Craft, or ALC, later known as the Landing Craft Assault (LCA), was the only serviceable British landing craft in the early stages of the Second World War. It had its first experience of combat, rather bizarrely, while landing the French Foreign Legion in Norway in 1940, and showed great promise during the evacuations from Dunkirk and Crete. It took part in many commando raids and landed the first British and Commonwealth troops in North Africa, Sicily and Italy. It was a tried and tested design by the time of the Normandy invasion, when it became the unsung hero. Boats commanded by leading hands or able seamen picked their way through beach obstacles to land the first waves of infantry, while more imaginative types of vessel such as the swimming tank, the Landing Craft (Rocket) and the Landing Craft Tank (Armoured) proved far less successful. It was still in service for the Suez operations in 1956.

The assault landing craft was the humblest vessel in the wartime Royal Navy during the Second World War. It was commanded by a rating rather than an officer, it did not appear in the *Navy List*, it had no armament of its own and it had a number rather than a name. It had no accommodation for cooking or sleeping so it was not expected to be used independently. It might be regarded as equivalent to a ship's boat, except that it was usually organised in flotillas and it was a true fighting vessel, not a support craft. It was certainly not pretty, in an age when the world had not yet become familiar with box-like vessels. Even in its role in amphibious operations, it tended to be dwarfed both literally and figuratively by larger vessels that could put tanks ashore with a certain amount of dramatic effect.

Nearly 2000 were built and these were a vital link in allied wartime operations. If each landed its full complement of thirty-five men only once, that would make a total of nearly 70,000. But if the average craft carried out four or five landings in action conditions, then they would have landed around 300,000, perhaps even more, and it is quite possible that half a million soldiers had the experience of the short but uncomfortable and dangerous voyage onto a beach held by the enemy.

American troops embarking into an LCA from a liner during the North Africa landings.

INCEPTION AND DESIGN

EARLY LANDING CRAFT

Most British wars, ever since the Norman Conquest, have involved some sort of combined operations between land and sea forces, such as in the countless colonial expeditions during the wars between Britain and France from 1689 to 1815. They were rarely opposed strongly on the beaches, but a notable exception was at the landing in Egypt in 1801. They mostly employed ordinary boats launched from ships, with the occasional use of specially designed flat-bottomed landing craft, such as the forty-nine wooden horse-boats that amused holidaymakers during army exercises at Clacton in 1904. They had ramps in the bows but they were to a thirty-year old design – the best that was available. It was not considered possible to invade in the teeth of strong opposition, so it was assumed that the landing would be unopposed.[1] The 1914–18 war produced only the Gallipoli landings, which were disastrous due to faulty doctrine and inadequate equipment. This tended to reinforce the growing view that such operations were impossible against modern weaponry. The enemy could defend long stretches of beach with machine guns and long-range artillery, while aircraft could detect any landing early and break it up on the way over. Moreover, an army would now have to arrive with supporting tanks and other vehicles, and the fuel to sustain them. Nothing was done to develop landing craft in Britain during the 1920s, except to produce the first Motor Landing Craft (MLC), which was a poorly designed vessel:

> With the wind in the right direction they would do five knots, the jet-propelling [i.e., water jet] engine was a bit temperamental and much preferred a short journey to a long one, it would carry a 6-inch gun without its mountings, and a row of mules or ten tons of stores. Short wheel-based vehicles found it impossible to get out over the bow because of the acute angle of the ramp with the deck, but that did not matter as the craft drew four feet six inches of water and vehicles in those days were not designed to land in any depth of water. From the personnel-carrying point of view it had no armour and was so noisy that no tactical surprise could be hoped for if the beach was manned by the enemy. She weighed twenty tons, and, because of her egg-like undercarriage, was not really at home on the flat deck of a merchant ship.[2]

THE WORK OF THE ISTDC

Prospects of war with Germany grew when the Nazis came to power in 1933, but that did not seem to create much demand for amphibious operations with France as an ally. Italian expansionism did, however, cause fears of a war in the Mediterranean, while Japan used its own landing vessels to invade China. In September 1938, the Inter-Service Training and Development Centre (ISTDC) was set up with headquarters at Fort Cumberland in Portsmouth. It consisted of one officer from each of the services, with a Royal Marines captain as adjutant. Captain L E H Maund of the Royal Navy had already helped draw up the official manual of combined operations and was to be its chairman. The ISTDC was to be 'responsible for the study and development of material, technique and tactics necessary for the success of opposed landings'. Later, this was amended so that it did not just include opposed landings. In December 1938, its detailed aims included provision of material for training. A special landing craft carrier was not considered essential yet, although 'One self-propelled landing craft should be constructed for experimental purposes and a report made on the results of the trials before further construction was ordered.' The provision of support landing craft was held in abeyance but trials were to be made on the use of 2in mortars in other craft. There were to be experiments in the use of infrared rays to guide craft onto beaches, with naval gunfire support for landings, the use of piers and

A horse boat, an ancestor of the LCA, as used in exercises at Clacton in 1904.

pontoons to help the discharge of stores, and the landing of troops from aircraft, so that both Mulberry harbours and paratroopers were considered at this early date.[3]

Meanwhile, an exercise at Slapton Sands in Devon turned into farce. The warships had to come close inshore so that the troops could be disembarked in ship's boats and rowed ashore, like their ancestors had been in the days of Drake and Nelson, without any armoured vehicles, artillery or motor transport. The general in charge refused to believe the weather forecasts and re-embarkation proved impossible – the troops had to march six miles through a gale to spend the night in the Royal Naval College at Dartmouth

With no practical experience of amphibious warfare, the committee had to theorise about tactics. Asked to design craft for landing troops on beaches, the ISTDC looked at the best size of vessel. In fact the Deputy Chiefs of Staff, who had set up the organisation, had already offered views and had formulated a requirement for 'special self-propelled boats carried in special carrier ships and launched one to two miles off shore in order that the assaulting infantry could attain a certain amount of surprise'. It was envisaged as 'having a small silhouette, capable of carrying forty fully equipped men and having a speed of 8-10 knots'. However, the ISTDC considered using the smallest possible unit – the eight-man section – as the basis for the landing craft for the first wave and:

> … from the point of view of the passage to the beach, it would be desirable that the unit carried in a landing craft should be as small as possible, i.e. a section. Unless the craft, and so the unit, is small, tactical surprise may be sacrificed. Should surprise be lost, casualties are likely to be heavy unless the first flight is dispersed into as many units as possible.

It is however doubtful whether a craft capable of negotiating the kind of sea that may be breaking on the beach would, with economy, carry less than a platoon.

The ISTDC considered whether the craft launching the second wave should be different from the first:

… it would be an advantage if the second flight could be sent in in as big units as possible. On the other hand, speed in reinforcement will be essential, and the larger the craft, the lower will be their speed. Casualties also are likely to be less if the second flight strike the beach in a number of small fast craft rather than a few large ones. They will certainly need protection against the defenders who, at least, will have been alarmed by the landing of the first flight.

Far-sighted as always, the committee was close to evolving the design of the Landing Craft Infantry (Large), which could land up to 200 troops during the later waves of an invasion. But for the moment it wisely decided to concentrate on a single type of assault craft for personnel:

> It is therefore considered that the second flight should be landed by platoons in craft of the same design as those used for the first flight. Armoured protection against machine gun fire will, however, be more necessary for craft in the second flight than for those in the first flight.[4]

At the other extreme, the upper limit on the size of the landing craft was determined by the need to carry it on board ships. The ISTDC would have preferred the Admiralty to build military transports with davits to carry fourteen landing craft, and with a speed of twenty-five knots, but this was always unrealistic with limited budgets and in practice merchant ships would have to be converted when war started. Nearly all ocean-going passenger ships carried ninety-nine-person lifeboats on davits, and it would be a simple matter to replace these with landing craft in wartime. Therefore the assault landing craft should weigh no more than ten tons.

DESIGNING AN ASSAULT LANDING CRAFT

The ISTDC applied to the Admiralty for help in formulating the design, but it was too busy with other projects. It turned to the Board of Trade, which, among other things, regulated merchant ship safety, and was referred to Fleming of Liverpool, a designer of ship's lifeboats. Fleming was an innovative and well-respected company, which had produced boats with crank handles so that the passengers could take turns at powering in an emergency. Fleming took up the landing craft idea with great enthusiasm and produced a plan by November.

The Fleming design was rather odd by any standards. The keel was almost completely straight, with an upwards curve in the bows and the stern rising to protect the propellers. In cross section, it was square in midships, with rounded bilges, and it altered to a much more rounded section, and triangular at the bow and stern. The central area, where the troops were carried, had a superstructure with plates angled inwards, and a flat structure between them. Its engines were fitted towards the stern, with a rectangular covered steering position between. From its experience in lifeboats the builders had gone for lightness by building it

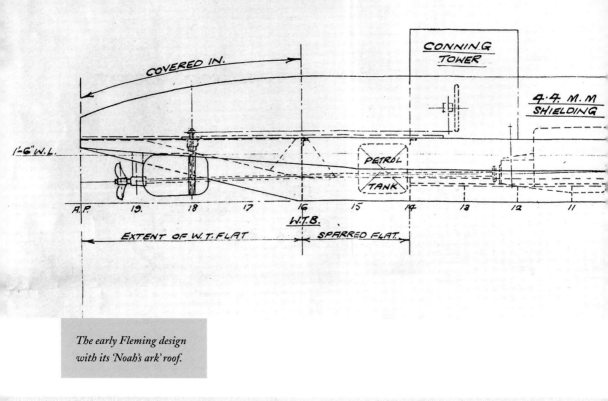

The early Fleming design with its 'Noah's ark' roof.

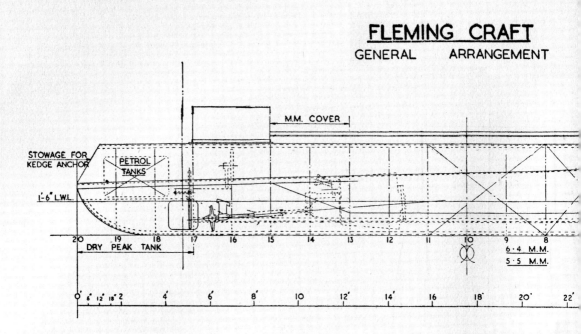

FLEMING CRAFT
GENERAL ARRANGEMENT

The final design of the Fleming boat.

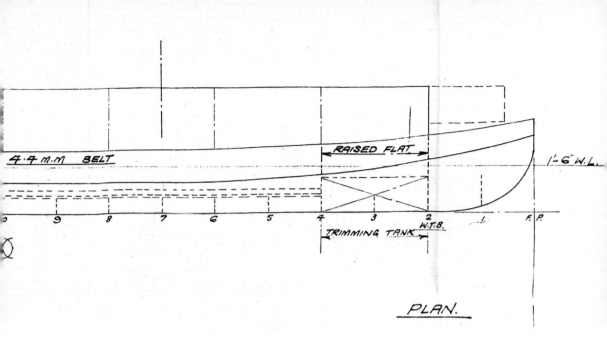

44 M.M BELT

RAISED FLAT

1'-6" W.L.

10   9   8   7   6   5   4   3   2   1   F.P.

W.T.B.

TRIMMING TANK

PLAN.

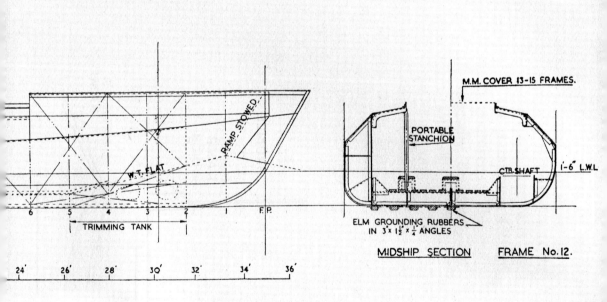

RAMP STOWED

M.M. COVER 13-15 FRAMES.

PORTABLE STANCHION

W.T. FLAT

CTR.SHAFT

1'-6" L.W.L

6   5   4   3   2   1   F.P.

TRIMMING TANK

ELM GROUNDING RUBBERS
IN 3" x 1½" x ¼" ANGLES

24'   26'   28'   30'   32'   34'   36'

MIDSHIP SECTION   FRAME No. 12.

in 'Birmabrite', an aluminium alloy produced by Birmal Boats of Birmingham and Southampton and used for lifeboats and motor yachts. The craft was thirty-five feet long, nine feet wide and had a depth of four feet from the keel to the top of the shelter.

On 21 November, Fleming's drawings were presented to a meeting convened by the Director of Naval Equipment, and which was also attended by the construction and engineering departments of the Admiralty, and the Royal National Lifeboat Institution. They were 'generally concurred in' and the Admiralty was asked to approve a mock-up to be made in Portsmouth Dockyard. According to Maund, 'We tried fully-equipped troops embarking and disembarking from it, and altered its design to meet practical difficulties.' Tank tests were carried out, but as a result of these it was thought that it would not be sufficiently seaworthy in the conditions to be expected, perhaps because its freeboard was very low. Fleming was asked to think again and produced a slightly more conventional design, although still with the angled 'roof'. It had much higher freeboard, ramp in the bows, and seating for the troops on long benches running fore and aft. It was just over thirty-six feet long and drew one foot six inches of water.

Meanwhile, the Admiralty, which had control of ship design, insisted on introducing other shipbuilding companies into the process for competitive tendering. To Maund's annoyance, three were invited to a meeting but two showed no interest. The third, Thornycroft, responded quickly and had a proposal in hand within forty-eight hours. John I Thornycroft & Co. Ltd was a well-established firm with a great range of work for the Royal Navy, overseas navies, shipping companies and private owners. It had built many types of ship, including destroyers, torpedo boats, ferries, cargo ships, luxury yachts and record-breaking speedboats, and it also specialised in heavy road vehicles.

Thornycroft's plan was produced by K C Barnaby, its chief naval architect since 1924, and was ready by May 1939. Its layout was similar to the Fleming design, with engines aft and a control position between them. It was built far more conventionally in wood, mostly mahogany. Its hull was rather more rounded in profile, with distinct upward curves in the bows. Its cross section was much more angular than the Fleming boat, with an almost square section at midships and an almost flat bottom for most of its length, which was an economical way of getting as much weight as possible on a shallow draught. At the stern, the area around the propellers was recessed so that they could be raised as high as possible. It too had a bow ramp for the men to disembark, and a high superstructure that made it look even more like Noah's Ark than its rival. The troops were seated on benches across the hull, two on each side and there was a passage down the middle – the roof was at its maximum height over the passage, so that standing men could get out while still under cover. It was thirty-nine feet long overall and thirty-four feet on the waterline, nine feet six inches broad and had a maximum draught of one foot nine inches, although less than that in the bows.

TESTING

Budgets were still tight and there was still a good deal of scepticism about the need for combined operations, but the ISTDC ordered prototypes of both boats from its £30,000 budget. These were ready within eight weeks. The Fleming boat was tested on the River Clyde and taken to Langstone Harbour near Portsmouth for comparative trials with the Thornycroft product. Maund could see much in favour of it. 'The troops disembarked from the Fleming craft in a quarter of the time taken by those in the Thornycroft, the silhouette of the Fleming craft was lower, it created less disturbance at speed, and it beached better.' But it had two fatal snags. The Birmabrite construction created a hull that was 'a veritable sounding-board' and 'the noise from her engines was terrific'. Furthermore, her materials and complex hull shape would make it very difficult to fit armour. As to the Thornycroft boat, however, 'Armour could easily take the place of the outer mahogany planking.' Slowness of disembarking could be rectified by lowering the position of the bow ramp and the simple expedient of fitting fore and aft seating as in the Fleming craft. The 'Noah's Ark' roof could be removed to reduce the silhouette, and it was replaced by a flat deck over the heads of the troops sitting on either side of the vessel, although not over those in the centre, leaving a gap for men to run out. Armour was fitted after experiments in the Army School of Musketry at Hythe determined the best type and thickness, allowing for bullets ricocheting off the

An early version of the assault landing craft, with the steering position aft.

water, and for the fact that German bullets had 200 feet per second greater velocity than British. The engines were silenced so that they could not be heard twenty-five yards away. It was decided to develop the Thornycroft design and the first model was in the water by April 1940, just in time for its first service in Norway.

At the start of the war in September 1939, eighteen ALCs were on order. On the one hand, this was not nearly enough for any major operation, but, on the other hand, it was not considered feasible to build many more and put these into lay-up with no immediate objective in mind. It was suggested that a new design should be prepared, and which could double as a ship's lifeboat and a landing craft. Fleming began work on this, but there is no evidence that it took to the water.

The assault landing craft was the most concrete result of the work of the ISTDC, but it also produced a new type of mechanised landing craft (MLC), which owed something to the type of 1926 but was far superior and could land a sixteen-ton armoured vehicle. It served alongside the ALC in many ships and campaigns, because it could also be carried in a Landing Ship, Infantry, along with assault landing craft, although it needed heavy derricks rather than davits. It became known as the LCM(1) but it had a design flaw in that it carried its load above the waterline, which limited its stability. Later, it was largely superseded by the Anglo-American LCM(3), which could carry almost twice the load, including a Sherman tank. A report of 1950 highlighted other flaws in the concept:

> This craft can carry one large motor vehicle and two small vehicles. It can also carry a tank of up to thirty-five tons weight, or an equivalent in men and stores. It cannot be carried on davits and must therefore be brought to the assault area in LST(C) or on the deck of some MT ships. It is useful for operating in restricted waters. Owing to transportation difficulties it is unlikely to be used in large numbers in any operation. There is the additional disadvantage that it takes five hours to get seven LCM into the water from LST(C), in fair weather. It cannot therefore be used in the assault stage of an operation unless there should be a Landing Ship Dock (LSD) made available for their carriage.[5]

Tanks could be carried much more efficiently and in larger numbers in Landing Craft, Tank (LCT) and landing ships tank (LST), which made the journey all the way across and did not need to be hoisted out from a parent ship. In any case, there was a tendency for tanks to get much bigger and far beyond the capacity of any LCM-type craft that could be hoisted out. The LCM did find a role in bringing ashore unit transport and supplies in the second wave of an invasion, and in landing groups of up to one hundred men, such as regimental headquarters, which were better kept together. But for some reason the LCM captured the popular imagination – at least four different companies produced plastic kits of it – while none did the more common LCA. They also tended to favour its American equivalent, the Landing Craft, Vehicle and Personnel (LCV(P)). This was a well-designed craft, faster and more seaworthy than the

LCA, but without the armour plate that gave a good deal of confidence and security to the troops on board.

In contrast to the LCM, the LCA remained in production throughout the war and in service for a decade afterwards, and was at the forefront of every major amphibious operation. Unlike other landing craft, it did not go through several marks. The wheelhouse was moved forward and put on the starboard side early in its development in 1940, giving the helmsman a good view while at the same time lowering the silhouette. Armour plate was added to its upper decks after the experience of the Bruneval Raid in 1941. As one officer commented:

> We learned that it was desirable to have the decks of the ALCs, such as they were, armour-plated as well as the vertical sides. On one raid the poor lad of a stoker was killed at the engine controls by a stray bullet fired down at the craft on the beach from a cliff top.

But in 1950 it was still regarded as 'the principal means by which infantry can be landed direct on the beach in the assault', although it was felt that some capacity to land light vehicles would be useful in any new craft.[6]

Deck armour could be fitted retrospectively to older craft, and other amendments were mostly minor. A standard Combined Operations lecture later in the war suggested that the ideal assault boat should 'have a low silhouette, be silent and be fast and they must be proof against small arms, and have a shallow draft'. The lecturer agreed that 'These requirements have largely been met in the present assault landing craft.'[7] Considering that it was designed at a time when no one in Britain had any practical experience of modern amphibious warfare, it was a remarkable achievement.

Layout and Build

The hull

Seen in profile and out of the water, the assault landing craft had just a hint of the attractive lines that might be expected from a yacht builder such as Thornycroft. The deck had a very slight upward curve, or sheer, to help the bow meet the waves more effectively. The lower bow had a much steeper curve, in what was officially known as the 'sampan' style, perhaps based on Maund's experience in the Far East. It was intended to allow the craft to beach gently whatever the angle of the shore. From above, the ALC also had surprisingly attractive curves as the hull narrowed towards the bow, which of course was completely flat because of the need to fit a ramp.

From any other aspect, the ALC was undoubtedly angular, although not entirely box-like. Boatbuilders called this 'chine' construction, with very definite corners in the form of the hull. It was an extreme example of a shape common in fast power boats, of a type built by Thornycroft and other yards. Its bottom was not completely flat, and was angled slightly upwards on each side. This allowed it to hit the water more gently when pitching. Fore and aft wooden battens, known as barwales, were fitted under the hull to make the vessel lie level if it was aground. The sides of the boat were not vertical but angled slightly outward, helping create a righting motion if the vessel heeled to one side or the other. The transom that formed the stern, however, was completely flat and vertical. The shape of the bow was dominated by the ramp, angled forward at about forty-five degrees when in the stowed position at sea. It was four feet six inches wide so that two lines of men could get out simultaneously, and it was raised and lowered by means of a system of pulleys inside the hull. It had small rollers on its outer end to help when getting off a beach.

Internally, the space behind the ramp was raised above the level of the troop deck, and shut off from it at sea by armoured doors. In early models, the space on either side was filled with a buoyant material known as Onazote. Behind the doors was the troop compartment, which took up more than half of the length of the vessel. The men sat on three rows of fore and aft seats. The men of the middle row were exposed unless canvas awnings were fitted; those on the outside could find some shelter under the decks. Forward in this area, the coxswain's steering shelter was fitted on the starboard side, except in very early models or

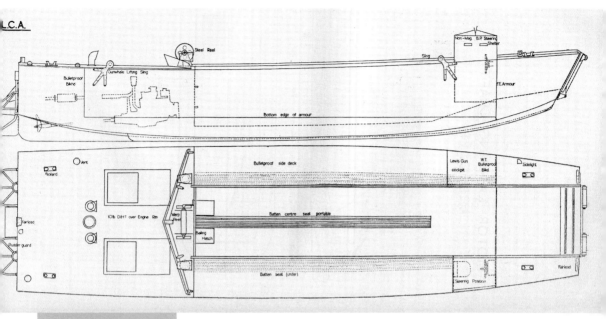

The outline plan of the LCA, giving prominence to the propeller guards and the central seat for the troops.

those adapted for special purposes. In that position it did not interrupt access to the troop accommodation, but it gave the coxswain a good view while keeping him low down. The steering position was armoured against small arms fire, with slots $1\frac{1}{4}$ inches wide that could be kept opened or closed. The coxswain had a folding seat fifteen inches above the deck, so he had a choice of positions. He could open the armoured doors on the roof to stand up and get a better view, or he could sit down, close the doors and get the benefit of the armour if enemy fire was intense. The coxswain had a car-type steering wheel and telegraphs for sending orders to the engine room, because he did not operate the engine speeds directly. He had two gear levers, one for each engine, and a voice pipe to communicate with the stoker. Selected vessels, to be used by flotilla leaders and navigators, had armour made in non-magnetic alloys so that they would not cause deviation on the compass. Later models had radios fitted just forward of the steering position.

On the port side, opposite the steering compartment, was an armoured position for a Lewis gun and later a Bren gun. This had full height armour forward, with its side panel sloping downwards, to allow the gun to be used for anti-aircraft fire. The frontal armour of this compartment, the steering compartment and the bow doors formed a continuous line against enemy fire. The deck of the troop compartment was mostly flat, except where it rose towards the bows to take the men to the armoured doors. The interior of the troop compartment was featureless except for the three benches, which were eight inches high and might be made with boards or slats. The central bench could be removed if stores were to be carried instead of men.

At the after end of the troop compartment was a watertight bulkhead that

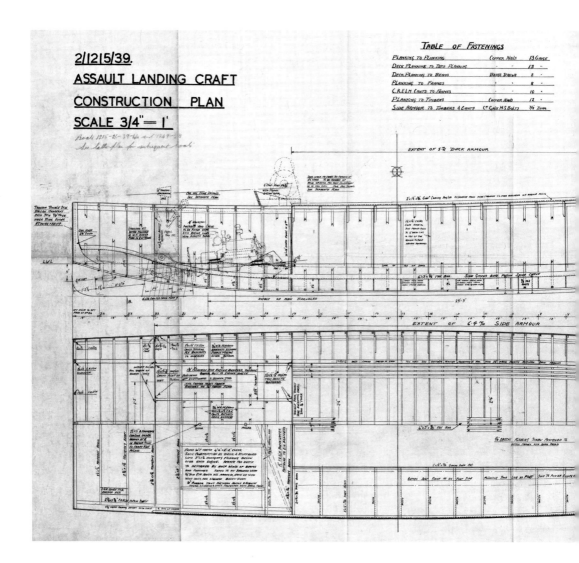

sealed off the engine room, with a small hatch for access by the stoker. Above this, the after deck of the craft covered the entire width and the engines. A small breakwater protected the crew and the troops from waves that might break astern. Just forward of that, easily accessible from the troop deck, was the anchor windlass. A small roller on top of this allowed the anchor cable to run free, and there was a double roller fairlead on the stern.

STRUCTURE

The basic structure of the assault landing craft was wood, mostly African mahogany, although other woods such as obechi, pine, teak and spruce were also used. Builders were enjoined to keep weight down by using no more wood than the specification demanded. The whole structure was based on a keel, $4\frac{1}{2}$ inches wide and made in Canadian rock elm. The hull was thirty-eight feet nine inches

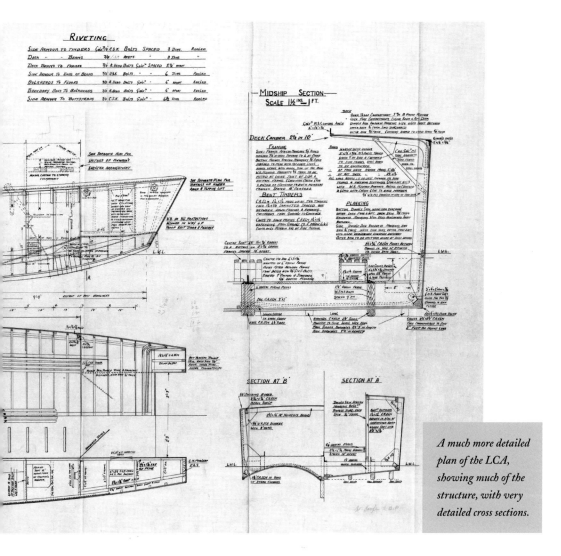

A much more detailed plan of the LCA, showing much of the structure, with very detailed cross sections.

long and its shape was provided by twenty-four mahogany frames, eighteen inches apart. These were covered by double diagonal skin planking, the layers of planks running in opposite direction to provide strength. The side planks were $\frac{1}{2}$ inch thick on each layer, with the bottom planks of $\frac{3}{4}$ inch. The structure was held together by copper rivets, brass bolts and brass screws. Steel armour was provided by the manufacturers already drilled with holes for fitting, so the hull had to be accurately constructed. The main armour on each side was 6.4mm or $\frac{1}{4}$ inch thick and ran from the bow doors to the after end of the engine room. It started just below the waterline. The specification for the first Thornycroft vessels was amended to include an armour plate over the engine room to protect the stoker, but after a telephone conversation with the authorities this was dropped to save weight – it was restored after several men were hit in action. In later boats, armour plate was also added to the decks to protect the troops below.

The completed frames of several craft in the Harris Lebus furniture factory in North London.

THE ENGINE

The engine room was roughly square in plan, with one Scripps V-8, a variation of a Ford design, on each side. The stoker sat between these engines to operate the controls, with a sixty-five-gallon petrol tank on either side. The positions of the escape hatches above him varied from model to model, either above his head or above the engines. He faced forward, with a view of various gauges and the engine room telegraph that conveyed orders from the coxswain. Electric power was provided for starting, but each engine also had a starting handle in a recess just forward of the engine room. It was geared to turn the propeller at a speed of no more than 1400 revolutions per minute. Each engine was angled slightly downwards to transmit the power to its propeller, and the hull around it was recessed in a 'semi tunnel', as the specification described it, to keep it high and the draught shallow. The engine room had a fire extinguisher that could also be operated from the steering compartment. The positions of the cowl ventilators to supply air to the engine, and the extractors to remove foul gases, also varied from time to time but these were to be found on the deck above. Exhaust gases ventilated through silencers over the stern by way of holes in the transom. They passed through a small after compartment, which contained nothing else but the gear to operate the rudders, and Onazote on early models. There were two rudders, one behind each propeller to give greater manoeuvrability and linked together by a rod inside the after compartment. These and the propellers were protected against grounding and debris by a complex system of iron rails erected around them. The anchor, a forty-five pounds patent model made by the Duerr company, was slung over the stern between the rudders.

A completed LCA showing the shape and fitting of the stern, the diagonal skin wooden planking and the armour plate which covers the sides.

Slinging

There were two ways of slinging the boat from its parent ship. For davits, there was a fixed slinging point above the after end of the engine compartment and another, stowed away flat when not in use, on the deck between the steering compartment and the gun shelter. Lifting by crane needed four points, and these were fitted to the outsides of the hull level with the other slinging points. Cleats were fitted on the decks at the bow and stern for conventional mooring alongside piers or other vessels. Ropes were hung along the sides of the boat to help any men in the water, dangling twenty-seven inches down from hooks twenty-four inches apart.

Unslinging often caused problems in bad weather, for example during the Sicily invasion, after which it was recommended to fit retaining plates at the top of the ring so that the hook would not fall over sideways, and to ensure that it would unhook quickly in a swell. Later ships had more sophisticated disengaging systems, such as Robinson's patent disengaging hooks. They also had bars between the davit falls that made the process of re-hooking the boat much easier.

Colours

Early boats were painted with three coats of black varnish on the inside of the bottom and three coats of service grey above the chine. Outside and below the waterline were two coats of grey undercoating and two of best quality grey enamel. Above the waterline were three coats of dark grey in the same pattern as used by the warships of the Home Fleet. During the evacuation from Greece in 1941, it was noted that the colour blended in with the local surroundings. In 1942, the first official camouflage scheme for the LCA was established by Admiralty Fleet Order. The bow was painted white, as were all features above the gunwale except the decks, which were dark grey. The sides had a wavy pattern of B30 or medium blue-grey paint. The bows had a V-shaped area of B30 down the centre to confuse observers about their shape.

In the same year, the Admiralty issued instructions on display of craft numbers on the stern and on both sides of the bow. The letter 'L' was to be eighteen inches high and six inches from the gunwale in the bows, painted with a white outline. The letters 'CA' were half that height, but the craft number went back to the height of eighteen inches. During the invasion of Sicily, it was noted that some flotillas painted additional numbers on boards to allow them to form up properly. This was 'strongly to be deprecated in future' because it might cause confusion and no craft should have more than one number. Nevertheless, craft used in the Normandy invasion also used a separate numbering system, known as the Landing Table Index Number, indicating their place in the operation. On Jig Green Beach, for example, the swimming tanks that were planned to land in advance of the assault were numbered *2004–2007*; the various types of landing craft, tank which came next were *2020–2028*, and the first wave of LCAs were numbered *2045–2054*, followed by *2070–2079* and *2085* and *2086*.

An assault landing craft under construction, painted by the war artist Leslie Cole.

THE BUILDING PROGRAMME

By June 1940, after some successes in Norway and at Dunkirk, there were forty-eight assault landing craft on order. The assistant chiefs of staff, looking to the defence of the country against invasion as their main priority, recommended 'that owing to the critical time and to the urgent need for destroyers, escort vessels, etc., no priority should be given to work on landing craft under construction and that no further construction should be undertaken' on the grounds that it was 'not considered as being immediately vital for the war effort'.[1] This did not match Churchill's view, for at the very same time he was setting up the Combined Operations organisation with Admiral Keyes at its head. By July, ninety-three LCAs were on order, although at this stage the Landing Craft, Motorised (LCM) was still considered suitable for large-scale use and 106 of these were on order. By February 1941, eleven ALCs were expected to be completed that month, thirteen in March and seventeen in April. By October, the rate had slowed to eight per month but it was to be increased to twelve; meanwhile the MLC was losing favour and only five a month were to be built, to add to the 188 ALCs and 119 MLCs in service.

An LCA is launched into the River Lea outside the Harris Lebus factory.

Thornycroft built many of the craft, but other firms, including its yacht-building rival Camper & Nicholson of Portsmouth, were soon drafted in to help. Thornycroft worried constantly about the demarcation of labour between the firms and their numerous subcontractors. By the beginning of December it was planned to have a total of 500 ALCs, with eight more to be ordered each month after that. The programme was greatly accelerated in 1942 after more than 200 had been built, and various non-marine firms, including joiners and furniture makers, were drafted in. These included Harris Lebus, a well-known company operating on the banks of the River Lea in North London, and which could launch the completed craft directly into the river. Some of the boats built by furniture makers leaked at first, but the result was generally found to be satisfactory. Much of the work in these companies was done by women. In total, 1929 LCAs plus several support landing craft were built.

3 CREWS

COMBINED OPERATIONS

Landing craft crews were part of Combined Operations, set up in mid-1940 with members of all three services. It was first commanded by Admiral of the Fleet Sir Roger Keyes, who had led the famous raid on Zeebrugge in 1918, but failed to reach the top as First Sea Lord in the 1920s. He had a tendency to bombard Churchill with unwanted advice and was succeeded by Lord Louis Mountbatten, a cousin of the King, in 1941. Mountbatten was rapidly promoted from captain to acting vice-admiral and built up the strength of the organisation. In 1943, he was replaced by General Sir Robert Laycock of the Royal Horse Guards, who had already gained considerable experience in commando raids, the evacuation from Crete and the landings on Sicily and Italy. He had far less public profile than his predecessors, but he was a highly efficient commander, the model for the admirable Colonel Tommy Blackhouse in Evelyn Waugh's *Sword of Honour* trilogy.

According to a secret memo of May 1942, 'The Chief of Combined Operations attends meetings of the Chiefs of Staff as a full member whenever major issues are in question and also, as heretofore, when his own Combined Operations, or any matters in which he is concerned are under discussion.' He was to advise all commanders-in-chief and force commanders on any combined operations they might carry out. He had senior officers of all three services under him, as well an inter-service staff headed by naval, military, Royal Air Force and Royal Marines advisers on combined operations. There was a signal section that co-ordinated the communications of the three services, and an intelligence section. By April 1943, Combined Operations had grown to nearly 44,000 officers and men, of which 28,000 were manning 2600 landing craft of various types.

At first, Combined Operations was envisaged as a raiding organisation, mostly using fast Landing Craft, Personnel (LCP) or R-boats, manned largely by ex-fishermen of the Royal Naval Patrol Service. By spring 1941, it was seen as a means of landing a mass army on the continent of Europe, and its tactics, personnel and equipment began to change. Patrol Service men were in short supply and were seen as too individualistic for the tight organisation needed for an invasion force. After that, landing craft crews were recruited from 'Hostilities

An LCA on the beach on Loch Fyne, near Inveraray.

Only' or HO men, who had joined the navy as conscripts or volunteers for the duration of the war, and mostly with no experience of the sea. There were very few regular Royal Navy officers and ratings in landing craft crews.

In the early days, the Combined Operations crews often lacked self-confidence and authority, as one Canadian seaman found:

> ... although clad in blue and paid by the Senior Service, nearly all the work is with the army. It is very difficult to tell where the Navy leaves off and the army takes on. On approaching an opposed beach, the Army and Navy officers together have to decide whether it is advisable to land or not, and each thinks of the other's problems before coming to a decision.[1]

CREW TRAINING

The LCA had a standard crew of four – a coxswain in charge, two seamen and a 'stoker' to operate the engines. The seamen usually came straight from the training bases around the coast where they were taught naval discipline and tradition, and the elements of seamanship and gunnery. The selection process was not in Combined Operations' favour at this stage, because many of the best men had already been creamed off as potential officers, technicians, signallers or asdic and radar operators.

The men came out of the basic training schools with the rating of ordinary seamen and were drafted to Combined Operations bases to learn about the operation and maintenance of landing craft. In the first half of 1941, there were signs of the constant tensions between different needs.

This period was marked by a conflict between two policies – the short-term plan of training for immediate raids, and the long-term plan to build up an efficient striking force. The short-term planners won the day and demands for craft crews to rehearse and stand by for particular raids, a great number of which were planned but most of which were cancelled, kept the number of craft available for training down to a very small number. There was also keen competition for the few craft available between the naval training establishment and the combined training centres, and in order to give the former a chance to catch up with the latter's requirements for trained crews, all combined training at the latter was suspended for three months during this period.[2]

By the end of 1941, 4500 men had been trained in landing craft of all types, and of these 1500 had been sent to the Middle East. Early in 1942, two holiday camps at Hayling Island were commissioned as *Northney I* and *Northney II*, and deck hands and coxswains did two weeks training there after which some were sent to HMS *Quebec* at Inveraray to form up into crews and start working with the army. Unfortunately, only a minority did this because *Quebec* only had accommodation for six flotillas and the rest were left to their own devices to become 'nobody's baby' – a common phrase in Combined Operations.

Even the training at Inveraray had a serious flaw, in that the half-trained crews soon exposed their weaknesses, and the army lost confidence in them. It was realised that each crew should be fully trained before any contact with the other services, although to a certain extent that remained an ideal because there was pressure for more and more men. However, facilities were increased with the opening a new basic training camp, HMS *Helder*, at Brightlingsea on the east coast of England. Seamen and coxswains were now given fourteen days of initial training in the form of lectures and demonstrations, and a similar time on the boats. Some were still sent to Inveraray, but the demand for operational crews created a severe shortage of instructors there. At the end of 1942, it was decided to cease minor landing craft training at Inveraray, and parallel courses were run at Brightlingsea and at Dartmouth, from where the Royal Naval College had then recently moved. Now the policy was to give two weeks initial training at Northney, followed by six weeks advanced training at Dartmouth or *Helder*. During the last two weeks, the men were formed into operational flotillas. Only then were selected flotillas sent to Inveraray, although the remainder went to holding or 'suspense' bases, where morale tended to drop and training standards fell.

> He next spends his time practising – for what? Operations that never seem to come off. Hope deferred and the results we know. These results are very much brought out in Combined Operations exercises and one frequently hears remarks form the Military that are anything but complimentary, and there is no doubt that the Military are justified. They have been led to expect the best of the Navy and when they are brought

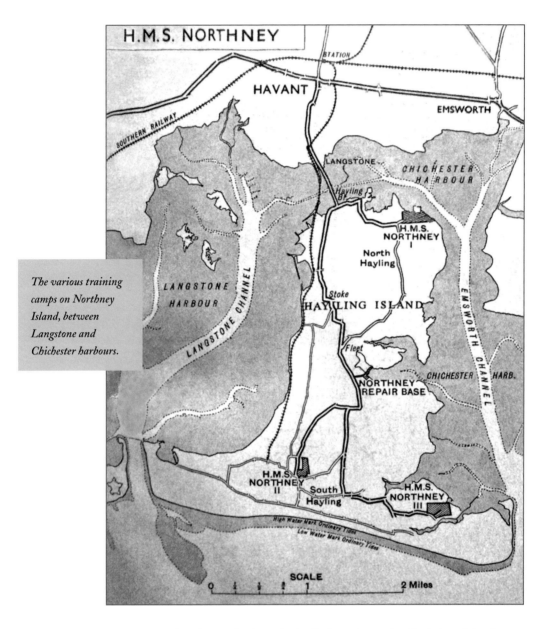

The various training camps on Northney Island, between Langstone and Chichester harbours.

up against these 'amateur' sailors who hardly know how to handle their craft let alone keep her clean, smart and shipshape, they certainly cannot be filled with confidence in their sister service.[3]

STOKERS AND SIGNALLERS

Stokers were trained separately. The title was of course a misnomer, from the days when most warships had been powered by coal. A modern stoker was a semi-skilled engineering mechanic and for Combined Operations purposes was trained for seven weeks at Northney in the operation and simple maintenance of all types of landing craft engine, although he would probably specialise in one type or another once he got to a flotilla. He attended classes in the principles of the internal-combustion engine, running the engine, the layout of an engine room, the hull of ship, fire fighting, maintenance, simple electrical systems, general operation such as clutch and gearbox and going astern, and the 'exhibition of awful warnings' such as propeller damage and the failure of a gear box, how they come about and how to avoid them.[4] He went to sea in the sheltered waters of the Solent, but that was not adequate preparation for the much rougher conditions that might be encountered outside. The stoker's most skilled task was starting and stopping the engine, which was quite a complex procedure. At sea he had to wipe electric leads occasionally, empty the bilges and carry out other simple tasks. The coxswain's orders were transmitted to him by engine room telegraph, and he had to vary the speed of each engine as required, or put it into reverse. He carried a simple toolkit, including adhesive tape and chewing gum for petrol leaks. On his right arm, he wore a badge of a three-bladed marine propeller.

It could be very unpleasant in the engine compartment of an LCA, especially for long periods. During the Dunkirk operation, the stoker of *ALC 5* became very depressed after more than fifty hours at the controls, breathing in the fumes from the crankcases and gearboxes, and was 'almost in a state of complete collapse'. It was rare for men to spend so long at the controls without relief, and improvements were made to the exhaust systems.

Landing craft signallers were also needed; one for each sub-division of three boats, who would carry out seaman duties as well as signalling. Each was trained to communicate by semaphore, torch, megaphone, and eight special flags were in use for particular signals. Only the officer's boat had a radio, so it was used to receive orders from above while other means were used to pass them on, and in any case radio silence had to be observed as far as possible.

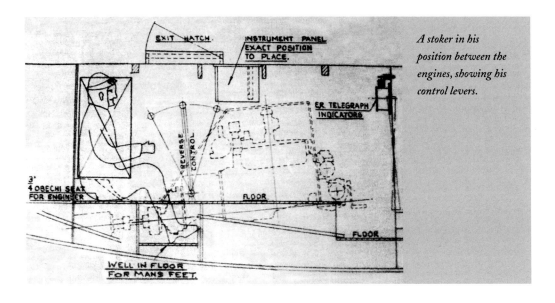

A stoker in his position between the engines, showing his control levers.

Coxswains

After six to twelve months of service, an ordinary seaman was eligible to pass for able seaman and be regarded as a fully trained man. In November 1941, the authorities considered it 'desirable' that coxswains of raiding and landing craft should be one step higher and have the rating of leading seaman, with an anchor badge on the left arm and some authority over the crew, but this was conditional on passing a fairly stiff examination. Candidates were questioned about the various types of landing craft in use, including their performance, load capacity and armour protection. They needed knowledge of signals and relative ranks with the army. Each had to do a practical test of his boat handling, including going alongside and mooring up, beaching by day and night, keeping station and steering a compass course for at least three miles, stopping and starting the engine. He also had to show he could use a range of weapons, knew how to stow his craft safely and could do simple first aid as well as demonstrating his 'power of command' over the crew. Charles Bowman was tested in this way:

> The test was to take command of a contingent of ratings on squad drill, on the Parade Ground, with a Royal Marine band playing a marching tune. To do this was no mean task, if I may say so. Anyway, I passed out. I had 87% for Power of Command, and 78% for Seamanship, which put me near the top of the passes, for seamen who took the examination. The rank of L/S/ Coxswain, gave me quite a promotion ... I had a boat and crew to look after, and be responsible for them.[5]

As always in the rapidly expanding world of Combined Operations, demand exceeded supply, and many coxswains remained as able seamen until they could pass for leading hand. During the Normandy invasion, ABs James Cole and

The crew of an LCA, headed by a petty officer coxswain. Most crews were less formally dressed than this on active service.

Daniel Ward commanded *LCA 1138* and *LCA 1375*, and were praised for their seamanship skills when things began to go wrong.

Coxswains had to be able to do all the tasks on board, and some officers encouraged all of the men to learn one another's jobs. An exercise for *Glengyle's* flotilla in 1942 was for each crew member to do one another's job in turn while the boats stayed in line abreast. Each coxswain was given quite extensive training in engine work so that he could take over if the stoker became a casualty, while in *Glengyle* each seaman had to take his turn at steering while picking up a buoy.

One perpetual problem was that good men were creamed off for other purposes. Some were sent for training as officers, while the best coxswains were taken away to do a very different job in a major landing craft – the senior rating on board under two officers, rather than taking charge themselves. Meanwhile, whole crews were drafted away on operations – the invasion of North Africa, Operation 'Torch', caused the diversion of both instructors and partly trained crews and there was no satisfactory cadre left in the training schools.

DISCIPLINE

Another problem, at least to the traditional naval officer, was that landing craft crews had little grounding in naval discipline. Conventional naval uniform, with the round cap, bell bottoms and square collar was worn for parades and going on leave, but rarely on board a landing craft. A dark blue version of the army battledress was issued, and also a khaki pattern for those who might find themselves ashore, such as in beach parties. But LCA crews, like many ratings in the wartime navy, tended to be rather informal and irregular in their dress, unless fear of capture caused them to wear full uniform. Practical items included the standard issue steel helmet, sea boots and a life vest, which was rather ineffective and was not compulsory.

Petty officers were quite rare in the LCA flotillas in the early days, because few regulars were drafted to the organisation and it took some time for HO men to reach that rating. However, in April 1942, *Glengyle's* flotilla had a petty officer for 'regulating' purposes – presumably an experienced regular attempting to enforce naval discipline. The flotilla's ten ALCs also had two more, one commanding a craft on each side of the ship. As well as taking charge of their boats, they were responsible for supervising the seamen in their work about the ship. The ship's two MLCs each had a petty officer, perhaps because of their larger crew of six men. The ship's two support landing craft each had a leading seaman as coxswain, but also carried a junior officer to direct its fire.

OFFICERS

Regular naval officers were equally rare in the landing craft flotillas. The great majority of junior officers were temporary members of the Royal Naval Volunteer Reserve (RNVR), who had joined the navy as volunteers or conscripts for the duration of the war in the rating of ordinary seamen and were selected for officer training. According to a report of 1943:

> It is perhaps forgotten now, but in the early days of the Combined Operations Organisation (1940 and 1941) an endeavour was made to build up the required forces without disturbing the rest of the Navy which at that time was hard pressed. This resulted in the organisation being manned and staffed almost entirely with Retired and R.N.V.R. Officers. This tended to give the impression that Combined Operations were a sideshow and caused difficulties when active service [i.e., regular] officers were superimposed on the R.N.V.Rs. who often had greater knowledge of the particular subject than the R.N. officers.

Hostilities-only seamen with a good education might be tested for three months at sea on the lower deck, and then given three months' training in naval techniques, discipline and administration at HMS *King Alfred*, a shore base near Brighton. On passing, they wore the 'wavy' stripes of the RNVR officers and were given a certain amount of choice in which branch of the service to join. Mountbatten found that very few applied for Combined Operations, so he made a point of visiting *King Alfred* himself and speaking to the trainees. He knew that the majority would always want to go to destroyers, and he had no difficulty with that. However, he persuaded many to put down Combined Operations as their second choice. Since there were few vacancies on destroyers, Combined Operations often got the cream of the new officers.

One who was recruited differently was Alisdair Ferguson, educated at Loretto School, Edinburgh, where he was head of school and captain of athletics, hockey, swimming, boxing and rugby. Finishing at *King Alfred* in autumn 1940, he volunteered for destroyers or motor torpedo boats but was sent instead to a flotilla of Yorkshire cobles, which were the subject of an early attempt to develop fishing boats as raiding craft. With LCA flotillas, he landed troops at Dieppe, 'the worst day of his life', in North Africa, Salerno and Normandy and was described as 'a natural born leader, with great aplomb and quiet courage'.[6] But not all officers could come up to this standard, and in September 1943 it was accepted that 'Although the selection is most carefully made the previous shortage of officers of Lieutenant's rank (now considerably improved) has meant the promotion of some officers who would not otherwise have been selected as flotilla Officers.'[7]

During the landings on Sicily, Major Peter Young had no confidence in the officer in charge of the flotilla:

> From first to last, everything went wrong. We were in the hands of the R.N.V.R. Officer commanding our landing craft flotilla who, if he knew his job, did not mean business. Perhaps he was merely incompetent. Conditions were not easy, with a strong head wind, a heavy swell and a black night.[8]

The other means of officer entry was through the Combined Operations base at Lochailort, in the Scottish highlands, commissioned in August 1942. Candidates for this course were often in Combined Operations already, and were selected for leadership and skill as much as education, while some had already failed the more formal course at *King Alfred*. Readers of the Combined Operations magazine *Bulldozer* were invited to:

> … use a little introspection and see if you find in yourself some of the qualities that are wanted, remembering that the Nation wants leaders and wants them now, and that it is your duty if you think you can achieve it, to give all that you have got towards the Service to which you belong and not to be content with the fact that you have done enough already.

They were warned, however, that the course was hard:

> … when you leave the train after, perhaps, a 20-hour journey, you will march into the camp and the candidates on course will tell you that you swim the Loch each morning, you climb the highest mountain before breakfast and, having dodged a couple of land mines, you work in an open lecture room for eight hours. This has a fair semblance of truth in it.

The six-week Lochailort course was very gruelling, with regular mountain walking and other physical exercises. It was designed to build up the men's stamina as well as teach them the rudiments of the skills they needed. Paul Lund, who did it, thought that:

> As seagoing officers in major and minor landing craft they would find that all their intensive physical training had been to little purpose. Most of their time at sea would be spent standing on the bridge of an LCT or LCI or in some minor landing craft; and the strain would not be so much physical as mental – keeping awake and alert for long periods of duty and being able to go for long periods without rest or sleep.[9]

A few regular naval officers were drafted in but they were not necessarily assets. After a rigid training as boys and long service in the big ships of the rather narrow-minded prewar Royal Navy, many did not have the flexibility of mind to take on their very different duties. At Dieppe, for example, one regular lieutenant-commander began by following the wrong gunboat inshore. He regrouped the flotilla then tried to make up time by allowing the lead boats to race ahead, leaving the slower LCMs behind. He headed for the entrance to the main port to establish his position, probably tipping off the enemy that something was happening, then headed east to his landing place at Puys. As a result, his forces landed thirty-five minutes late and the next wave was an hour late.[10]

THE FLOTILLA

The LCAs, like most landing craft, were organised in flotillas. The standard number of boats was twelve, but that might be modified according to the size of

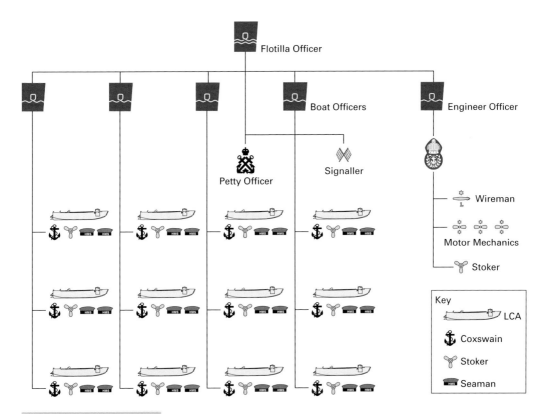

Flotilla Officer

Boat Officers

Engineer Officer

Petty Officer

Signaller

Wireman

Motor Mechanics

Stoker

Key

LCA

Coxswain

Stoker

Seaman

The typical organisation of an LCA flotilla.

the landing ship in which they were based. In their early stages, the *Glen*s had twelve LCAs, but this was later increased to twenty-four and each had two flotillas. Smaller LSIs had six or eight boats, perhaps with LCMs mixed together in a single flotilla. Each flotilla was headed by a lieutenant or lieutenant-commander, experienced by Combined Operations standards. Under him, each group of three boats had an officer, usually a sub-lieutenant with a single strip on each arm. Each boat officer was expected to take command of the craft he was in, but to leave the steering to the coxswain and to direct operations generally.

In addition to its four officers, a standard twelve-boat flotilla had a small staff for maintenance purposes. It had an engineer officer, a highly skilled engine room artificer and a semi-skilled stoker. It also had a wireman or electrician, four motor mechanics that (unlike most naval engineers of the time) had specialised in the internal-combustion engine, and a shipwright or joiner to repair the hull. The flotilla had no intelligence or administration staff; such work devolved on the officers or was carried out at the shore base or LSI, which had a strong administrative team.

MARINES IN LANDING CRAFT

By 1943, there was a manning crisis because practically all of the nation's young men had already been called up, while the landing craft organisation had to grow even faster. The Combined Operations organisation was allowed an intake of 3000 men per month up to 31 May 1943, after which all recruiting had to cease. In the meantime, the Royal Marines had expanded like other arms of the services, but its traditional role as part of the complement of battleships and cruisers was in decline. Under the command of Royal Navy officers, Royal Marines personnel began to serve in Combined Operations vessels by manning the armament of landing craft gun and flak. Soon, Royal Marines officers were given command of the craft, and it was only a short step when, in September 1943, it was decided that Royal Marines should form the crews of all minor landing craft, including LCAs – a 'somewhat revolutionary change', because they had always been subservient to the Royal Navy when on board ship. The Royal Marines Division was disbanded and its men were used to man minor landing craft such as LCAs, although they had to learn basic seamanship. In the meantime, existing naval crews were to be drafted into major landing craft, although this process was far from complete in 1944.

A complete new training organisation for the Royal Marines was set up, and was based in five camps in North Wales. Marines went to Matapan Camp near Towyn, where they were kitted out and assessed as potential coxswains, signallers, deckhands or engineers. The coxswains and deckhands then went to Gibraltar Camp near Llanegryn, where they did two weeks of intensive signals, seamanship, infantry and assault course training, even though they had already done full marines training. Engineers then went to Northney to train as the naval ratings had done before them, while the course intensified for coxswains:

> ... we had hardly any time to ourselves and what time we had was really taken up, for after the daily stint we were all too tired. As soon as one period of instruction was over there would be an officer or naval Petty Officer to take over. If Morse code training was followed by PT then one had only a few minutes to change. Seamanship would be followed by a talk on aircraft recognition, then someone else would talk to us on operating the Browning machine-gun and next instruction on Ford V8 engines. It seemed that the coxswains had to know everything that concerned landing craft and the running of them.[11]

After that, they went to Burma Camp at Llyngwril ('Little Willie' to the troops) for more advanced instruction, including tides and navigation, under strict discipline. They went on field exercises and trained on LCA simulators, 'just sitting at a wheel with all the controls and with the motions of being afloat'. They were also awarded the Combined Operations badge at this stage. From Iceland Camp near Arthog, they took actual boats out into the river, and had a practical demonstration of the effects of tides on the railway bridge at Barmouth, where unwary helmsmen might be trapped by the currents. After that they went to Dartmouth or Brightlingsea to be formed into flotillas and train with the army.

Engineers were considered to be 'of slightly higher intelligence than the stoker entry previously detailed for Combined Operations craft'. They were given a four-week course at Northney:

During the first week the men are introduced to the [internal combustion] engine and learn the elements of the engine and its system

In the second week the men pass to running engines (Gray Diesels, Hall Scott, Ford V8, Chrysler etc.) and learn the starting and stopping routine.

In the third week they learn about the Ignition, Water and Lubricating Systems etc., and they have instruction on the auxiliary machinery.

In the fourth week they have instruction on log books, fire extinguishers and drivers' duties, and some revision. Special films are shown of the running of I.C. engines and the work of Combined Operations.[12]

After that they spent three weeks afloat, though mostly in the sheltered waters of the Solent, where they did not learn how to cope with seasickness.

ROYAL MARINES IN ACTION

Royal Marines were regarded as a success in manning minor landing craft, and formed about two thirds of the crews at Normandy in June 1944. The corps inspired a fierce loyalty and had a stricter disciplinary training than the Royal Navy, which pleased regular officers. The men were highly motivated and regarded as more intelligent than those from the naval training bases, who were not always the pick of the bunch. According to the report on the landings on Gold Beach in Normandy in 1944:

The Royal Marine craft crews, on the whole, fully justified themselves, particularly the L.C.A. flotillas which had a reasonable time for training and had more experienced officers. They had also worked together for several months in flotillas embarked in ships.[13]

They had good relations with the army and were more likely to take an interest in the land battle as it developed, although that was not an unqualified blessing. The beachmaster on Nan White in the Juno area during the Normandy landings complained that Royal Marines crews had a tendency to wander inshore and neglect their craft. During the same operation, all five craft of No 544 LCA flotilla were lost and Captain G S H Miers formed his men into a platoon, but nobody seemed to want them and they went back to the parent ship. In Yugoslavia in 1945, Lieutenant Davis was in charge of some LCAs on the beach waiting to withdraw commandos and he:

… organised the first five to reach the beach into a search party, armed them with marine rifles, and, without waiting for any more Commandos, or the troop officer to arrive set off to the village where the ambush had occurred to rescue the wounded, leaving the flotilla Engineer Officer in charge.[14]

The Royal Marines retain the role of manning minor landing craft up to the present day.

4 Parent Ships

Assault landing craft were not intended to operate for any length of time on their own and their design was based on the ability to be launched from standard ships' lifeboat davits. They had limited range, with no living accommodation, heads or cooking facilities – the only issue of food was an emergency ration of biscuits and tinned meat. It was very rare for them to operate without a parent ship within a few miles, although No 48 Royal Marine Commando did so among the islands of Zeeland in spring 1945, while others co-operated with naval and land forces among the Yugoslavian islands in the same year.

The *Glen* ships

After the experience of Norway in 1940 showed the value of small landing craft, the Admiralty looked for suitable ships to carry them. Three large merchant ships, *Glenearn*, *Glengyle* and *Glenroy*, were already in naval service. These had been designed just before the war for Glen Line Ltd, London, to operate scheduled services between Britain and the Far East, carrying cargo and passengers at a speed of eighteen knots. They were converted for Operation 'Catherine', an abortive attempt to enter the Baltic inspired by Winston Churchill as First Lord of the Admiralty, although many people continued to believe the cover story that they were to be used as supply ships for operation in the South Atlantic. They were converted again in summer 1940, with troop spaces in the hold and twelve ALCs slung from davits, plus three LCMs, which could be hoisted out more slowly from derricks. The ALC davits were of a merchant ship lifeboat standard type produced by the well-known firm of Welin-Maclachlan. Each boat rested on a cradle that was part of the davit, and on use the davit was angled outwards and the boat descended by gravity. Winches were provided to hoist it back. Although the davits had been built to cope with the ten tons of a passenger ship standard lifeboat, they were strengthened during the refit. This was fortunate, because the load of an ALC tended to increase over the years. The ships had only defensive anti-aircraft armament because they were expected to operate with a naval escort. *Glengyle* had two 12-pounder guns, eight 2-pounder pompoms and four machine guns. According to one of the crew she was 'a strongly plated ship of thick steel, made to take a buffeting'.[1]

As first fitted out for naval service, the *Glen*s were planned to carry a ship's

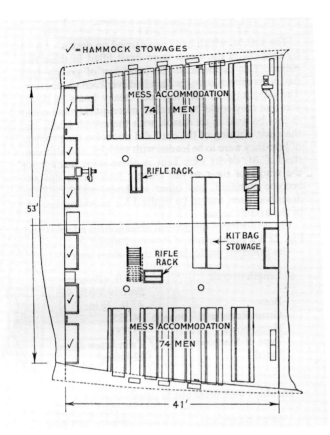

✓ = HAMMOCK STOWAGES

MESS ACCOMMODATION
74 MEN

RIFLE RACK

53'

KIT BAG
STOWAGE

RIFLE
RACK

MESS ACCOMMODATION
74 MEN

41'

*A typical troop mess deck
on one of the* Glen *ships.*

crew of twenty-eight officers and 263 men plus twelve officers and 220 men for landing craft crews, which allowed a substantial margin for casualties and fatigue in operations. They could carry eighty-seven army officers and 1000 men – equivalent to an infantry battalion plus supporting troops. The troops on board *Glengyle* lived on six decks, all aft of the funnel. The largest mess was equipped for 158 men to sleep in hanging billets or hammocks, while up to 256 could be seated for shorter voyages that did not involve an overnight passage. The smallest mess, No 5, had eighty-six hanging berths and 136 seats. In total, there were sixty-five mess tables, and two or three might be combined to accommodate a platoon. The sergeants were allowed the use of three tables on No 1 troop deck, but they had little privacy – they did far better in ships such as *Keren* and *Karanja*, in which they shared cabins in the second-class accommodation.

The officers, as usual on ships, had far better accommodation, in single or double cabins. This did not prevent conflict between the navy and army officers on board, especially when 8 Commando was taken round the Cape of Good Hope to Suez in 1941. The army included several well-connected gentlemen including the sons of both Winston Churchill and Sir Roger Keyes, as well as the acerbic novelist Evelyn Waugh. They had to share the wardroom, but the army officers believed that they were first-class passengers and the navy was the equivalent of a guard on a train.

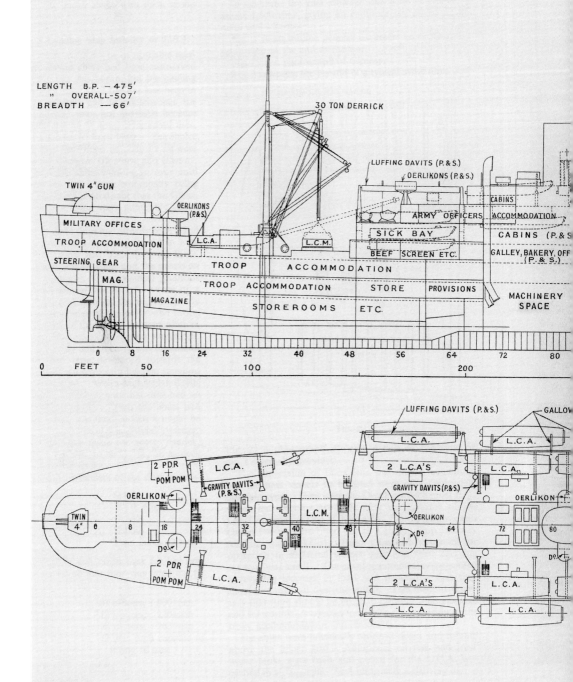

LENGTH B.P. — 475'
" OVERALL—507'
BREADTH —66'

30 TON DERRICK

LUFFING DAVITS (P. & S.)

OERLIKONS (P. & S.)

TWIN 4" GUN

CABINS

OERLIKONS
(P & S)

ARMY OFFICERS ACCOMMODATION

MILITARY OFFICES

CABINS (P. & S

SICK BAY

TROOP ACCOMMODATION

L.C.A.

L.C.M.

GALLEY, BAKERY, OFF
(P. & S.)

BEEF SCREEN ETC.

STEERING GEAR

TROOP   ACCOMMODATION   STORE   PROVISIONS

MAG.

TROOP ACCOMMODATION

MACHINERY
SPACE

MAGAZINE   STOREROOMS   ETC.

0   8   16   24   32   40   48   56   64   72   80

0   FEET   50   100   200

LUFFING DAVITS (P. & S.)   GALLOW

L.C.A.   L.C.A.

2 PDR
+
POM POM

L.C.A.

2 L.C.A'S

L.C.A.

GRAVITY DAVITS
(P. & S.)

GRAVITY DAVITS (P. & S.)

OERLIKON

OERLIKON

TWIN
4"   0   8   16   24   32   40   48   56   64   72   80

L.C.M.

OERLIKON

Dº

Dº

Dº

2 PDR
+
POM POM

L.C.A.

2 L.C.A'S

L.C.A.

L.C.A.

L.C.A.

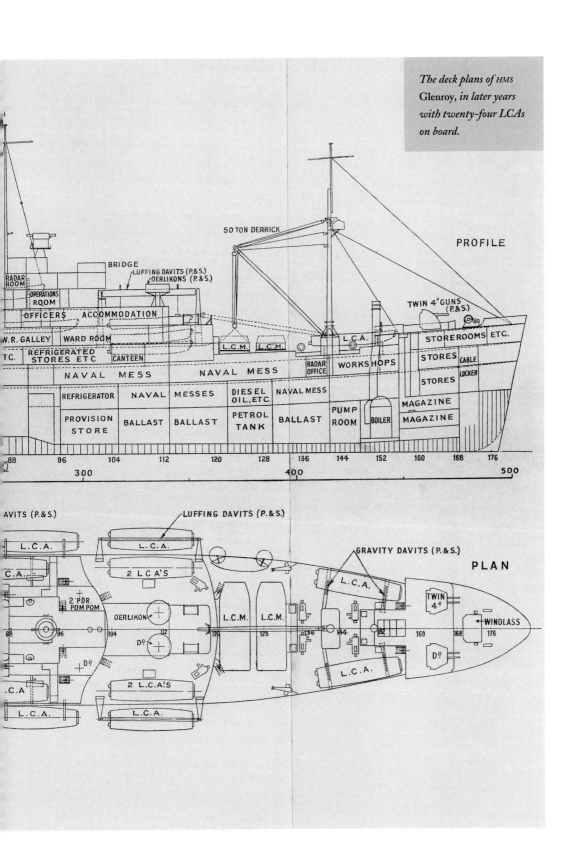

The deck plans of HMS Glenroy, *in later years with twenty-four LCAs on board.*

PROFILE

50 TON DERRICK

BRIDGE
LUFFING DAVITS (P.&S.)
OERLIKONS (P.&S.)

RADAR
ROOM

OPERATIONS
ROOM

OFFICERS ACCOMMODATION

TWIN 4" GUNS
(P.&S.)

W.R. GALLEY | WARD ROOM

L.C.A.

STOREROOMS ETC.

TC. | REFRIGERATED
STORES ETC | CANTEEN

L.C.M. | L.C.M.

RADAR
OFFICE | WORKSHOPS

STORES | CABLE
LOCKER

STORES

NAVAL MESS | NAVAL MESS | STORES

REFRIGERATOR | NAVAL MESSES | DIESEL
OIL, ETC. | NAVAL MESS | MAGAZINE

PROVISION
STORE | BALLAST | BALLAST | PETROL
TANK | BALLAST | PUMP
ROOM | BOILER | MAGAZINE

88 96 104 112 120 128 136 144 152 160 168 176

300 400 500

AVITS (P.&S.)

LUFFING DAVITS (P.&S.)

GRAVITY DAVITS (P.&S.)

PLAN

L.C.A.

L.C.A.

C.A.

2 LCA'S

L.C.A.

TWIN
4"

2 PDR.
POM POM

OERLIKON

L.C.M. | L.C.M.

WINDLASS

Dº

88 96 104 112 128 136 144 152 160 168 176

Dº

Dº

.C.A.

2 L.C.A'S

L.C.A.

L.C.A.

L.C.A.

IMPROVEMENTS TO THE *GLENS*

By April 1942, experience had shown that sixteen ALCs and two support landing craft were needed to land an infantry battalion and supporting troops, and none of the LSIs had that many craft. Furthermore, the latest ALCs weighed twelve to thirteen tons instead of ten, and the existing davits were under severe strain. All of the *Glen*s were refitted during the year, with a different design of davit and a larger number of craft. A new type of davit was fitted, much stronger and with a cross-bar over the top. Two boats could be stowed under it, with a third suspended just outside the hull. Four of these groups were fitted in positions forward and aft of the main superstructure on either side. In addition, four more boats were fitted outside the hull on gallows davits opposite the main superstructure, while those on the older davits there and at the bow and stern were retained, giving a total LCA complement of twenty-four. Three LCMs were also carried.

Accommodation was increased at the same time. Dormitory cabins were provided for some of the junior officers, while cooking, storage and ventilation facilities were improved. An operations room was fitted near the bridge, with access to signals and radar. Armament was increased to three 4in guns, four pompoms and eight 20mm Oerlikons, and fire control was improved. A well-equipped workshop was fitted for the maintenance of landing craft, which were already proving vulnerable to damage during landings.

The *Glen*s were among the hardest worked ships of the war. At least one took part in every major landing operation as well as several minor, and they trained for others that never took place. Although not designed for the role from the keel up, they had the right capacity and speed for amphibious operations. None was lost, although they were 'torpedoed, mined, bombed, burnt or stranded; they survived, struggled home and, repaired and refitted, finished the war as staunch as ever'.

THE SMALLER SHIPS

Other merchant ships were converted later in 1940 – all much smaller than the *Glen*s. Ferries that operated to the Netherlands were obviously redundant now that their country was occupied, so two, *Princess Beatrix* (formerly *Prinses Beatrix*) and *Queen Emma* (formerly *Koningin Emma*) were taken over for Landing Ships Infantry (Medium). They had been designed only for sheltered waters, so they needed more conversion than the *Glen*s. Each carried six ALCs and two LCMs on davits along the sides, with twenty-two army officers and 350 men as the normal load. This did not match any standard army formation, unlike those carried by the *Glen*s.

Belgium was also in enemy hands and six ferries – *Prins Albert*, *Prins Phillipe*, *Prince Charles*, *Prince Leopold*, *Prinses Josephine Charlotte* and *Prinses Astrid* – were taken over for conversion to LCI (Small), mainly with raiding in mind. The first two had diesel engines instead of the older steam turbines and proved more

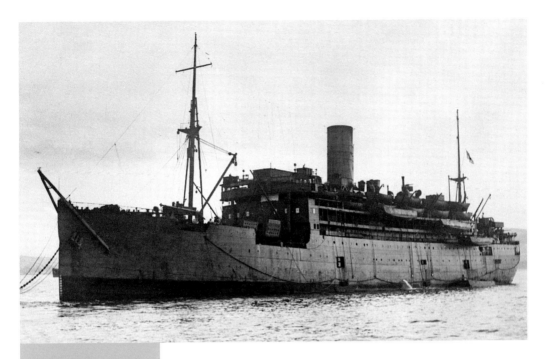

efficient in service. They were slightly smaller than the Dutch ships but the landing craft complement was kept up to eight by substituting ALCs for the two LCMs of the Dutch ships. A seventh Belgian ferry, *Prince Baudouin*, was taken over in 1943 after *Prins Phillipe* was sunk in an accident.

Several British ferries, designed to operate to France, the Isle of Man, the Channel Islands or Ireland, were also taken over. *Ulster Monarch*, *Royal Scotsman* and *Royal Ulsterman*, for example, differed from the Dutch and Belgian ships in that they were fitted with extensive cabin accommodation rather than promenade decks. This allowed more space for troops, but it was difficult to fit davits in the same way. Boats were carried outboard on spurs and had to be raised by manual winches – hence the ships were known as LSI(H), for hand hoisting. They were used for short-range missions and could carry troops for a maximum of forty-eight or ninety-six hours. They were obviously improvisations, but continued in service throughout the war.

As the need for amphibious operations intensified, yet more ships were taken over. *Karanja* and *Keren* were also fast eighteen-knot passenger and cargo ships designed for Far Eastern service by British India Steam Navigation Company, London. *Keren* (then in her original name of *Kenya*) had carried three LCAs during the abortive Dakar expedition of 1940 and, with *Karanja*, she was more fully fitted during the second half of 1941, although it was still regarded as a rather basic conversion. She served as headquarters ship as well as landing ship for the invasion of Madagascar in 1942, along with her sister. *Prince David* and *Prince Henry* were acquired from Canada in late 1942 and were manned by Canadian personnel in the first instance. They were well fitted out, with a good armament and communication facilities. By the time these came into service, there was no need to carry LCMs because other vehicle-landing vessels were available, which made conversion easier.

Red Ensign ships

In 1943, the government took over under lend-lease a dozen standard merchant ships of the C1-B class building in the United States, and these were converted to LSI (Large), to be operated by merchant navy crews. These were quite well fitted with recreation spaces and a cafeteria for 1300 troops, eating in shifts. Instead of hammocks, the soldiers lived in American style 'standee' bunks three or four high with the upper bunks folded away in the daytime. Up to eighteen landing craft could be carried. Some officers, however, objected to the merchant navy crews, and relations between the Royal and merchant navies were often quite difficult. In the run up to the Normandy invasion, the crew of *Empire Mace* went on unofficial strike because some of the lifeboats were replaced with landing craft. The naval officers on board *Tegelberg* became confused when her status was changed from troopship to Landing Ship Infantry (Large), the rival Protestant and Catholic chaplains had to vie for space, and the Merchant Navy master undermined the naval officers by suggesting openly that lowering exercises were not carried out properly. The ship was alcohol-free because she was carrying American troops, which increased friction even more. Another officer complained that merchant seamen resented being kept on board while the ship was at anchor in a home port, although it was necessary because of security. He felt that '... an operation of this sort cannot risk a part of the Force refusing duty or not being available owing to the indiscipline of a few ignorant and dissatisfied men'.[2]

In addition to the normal equipment of a troop-carrying ship, a fully fitted Landing Ship Infantry needed suitable radio equipment and perhaps an operations room, store rooms, a landing craft workshop, a flotilla office, a control room for disembarking troops, a broadcasting and telephone system to control the process, petrol storage and scrambling nets down the side. The fitting of the ALCs varied from ship to ship. In *Keren*, *Karanja*, *Winchester Castle* and *Sobieski*, the craft were lowered and hoisted in two stages because the davits had not been specially converted.

Troops on board

On arrival on board a landing ship, the troops were allocated to the decks for sleeping and eating, and had the standing orders read to them. On the *Glen* ships, each was issued with a hammock, although not a mattress to go inside it as the sailors used, and the army was expected to supply him with blankets. A senior NCO was put in charge of each troop deck. Every group was responsible for the cleanliness of its own deck, and men were detailed to clean the passages. Other parties were chosen to work in the galley, bakery and canteen. Training took place during a long voyage out, under the orders of the officer commanding the troops.

This might vary even with two forces in the same ship. According to Evelyn Waugh in *Glenroy* on the way to Egypt as an officer in No 8 Commando, his colleagues in No 11 Commando 'trained indefatigably during the voyage. We did very little except PT and one or two written exercises for the officers.'

Major Plowden of the Royal Engineers commented:

> The soldier in battle order takes up an extraordinary amount of space … the minimum width of any companionway or alleyway should be about 12 feet! It has been found extremely difficult to marshal troops at their action stations as it is nearly always necessary for troops to pass through troop spaces other than their own …
>
> More adequate drainage should be provided in troop spaces and latrine accommodation; few people who have not seen them can have any idea of the indescribable mess which these places become in rough weather. …
>
> Then a most important point is sea kindliness. … one of my main worries was not that the gale would interfere with the physical act of landing, but that the troops would be in no condition to work when they got to the beaches on account of seasickness.[3]

LAUNCHING THE LCAs

On an operation, the landing ships would assemble at the lowering position off the coast they were about to attack. The standard distance from the shore was seven miles, but that might be varied according to the depth of water, the need for surprise and the possibility of enemy activity. If possible the ship anchored with her bows pointing to the shore. Lowering the first flight from the davits also involved a large part of the crew of the parent ship. In 1942, *Glengyle* needed two lowerers on each of the LCA davits, plus seventeen more men for the LCM derricks, and communications ratings and messengers to a total of fifty-four. The captain complained that he did not have enough men to do that and man the ship's anti-aircraft guns at the same time.

A standard lowering drill had evolved by 1943. The order 'operation stations' was piped through the ship's loudspeakers and the boats crews went to their craft while the troops stayed on the mess decks. Then 'boats to embarkation level' was piped and they were lowered to a suitable height, while the troops got ready to embark. On 'man the boats', the sailors helped the soldiers on board. When that was complete, and checked by the flotilla officer and adjutant of the infantry battalion, 'craft ready and manned' was reported to the bridge. The order 'lower way' was given and the first flight took to the water.[4]

During the attack on Anzio in 1944, a few LCAs were carried into action by Landing Ship Tank (LST) fitted with davits and it was suggested that they might make the LSI obsolete for short-range operations, but they came into their own again during the Normandy invasion. In total, more than fifty ships served as LSIs during the war, all converted from merchantmen because there was no time to design and build such ships from scratch. Thirty-seven were present off the British beaches during the invasion of Normandy in 1944, and eight more British manned LSIs were in the American sector.

The decks of the Empire Mace *during an exercise before the Normandy invasion, with an LCA just visible on the davits to the left.*

5 TECHNIQUES AND TACTICS

HANDLING

The LCA, like most landing craft, did not handle like a conventional vessel. Its flat bottom, flat sides and shallow draught made it very susceptible to leeway or being pushed to one side or the other by the wind. It was slightly less vulnerable than its American counterpart, the LCV(P), because of its lower sides, but it was always a factor that had to be taken into account. The LCA was also very manoeuvrable. The engines could be turned in opposite directions to give a strong rotating motion, and the rudders were set behind the propellers to give turning maximum effect from a burst of power. However, coxswains were discouraged from using too much power in reverse because the rudder guards did not sufficiently protect the water intakes from debris and sand. Coxswains also had to remember that a craft would continue turning unless the helm was turned in the opposite direction to stop it. It took a good deal of practice, both with an individual boat and as part of a flotilla, to make the LCA efficient and relatively safe.

TRAINING IN SERVICE

The captain of *Glengyle* prepared thirteen different exercises to train his LCA crews. They could be awarded points for keeping station on one of the ship's cutters, while crew members changed around their jobs. One boat might pick up a mooring buoy and another would tie up alongside her and the second boat would take her in tow and bring her round to the other side of the ship, with marks awarded for 'style and method (including quietness)'. Relay races might be held around four boats moored together, with lifejackets optional. There were signalling exercises, handling exercises around buoys and beaching exercises. Boats could be timed in lowering from the davits, and in wading ashore with a line from a position fifty yards out on a beach.

Training became more sophisticated by 1942, when Force J was set up in the aftermath of the Dieppe raid. It was intended as a permanent raiding force based in the English Channel with its headquarters in the Royal Yacht Squadron at Cowes. Several LSIs with their flotillas were attached to it, but its existence was threatened from time to time, for example at the end of the year when nearly all the experienced crews were withdrawn to take part in Operation 'Husky', the invasion of Sicily. Soldiers, including the Canadian 3rd Division, were attached to it for training, and it became the nucleus of the force that invaded Juno Beach in Normandy in June 1944. It carried out numerous exercises, such as Operation 'Pirate' in October 1943, which was intended to provide 'Practice by an Assault Group in leaving harbour, making a passage, dawn rendezvous, and deployment in the Assault Formation.' The crews were carefully trained in what their commander believed was essential for a cross-channel attack – precise navigation, 'working to an accurate time table, in the face of strong tidal streams and complicated hazards, such as enemy minefields, etc.'; the 'ability to operate as part of a large and heterogeneous force by night and day in close company'; and the need to maintain discipline and aggressive spirit among both landing craft crews and troops. There was extra training and exercises in advance of a major operation, especially the Normandy landings:

Troops landing on a beach during an exercise in the Portsmouth area in May 1944.

... all the LCA crews were sent to Baseldon [Bursledon?] near Southampton. There was more extensive training of troops in full battle gear. We did have some casualties, some got out in rather high water, turned over and drowned owing to the weight they were carrying on their backs. We also had training in aircraft recognition, largely owing to the experience of Dieppe ... .[1]

The ultimate exercises were held in May 1944. In the series code-named 'Fabius', landings were carried out by each of the assault forces using all arms including army and air force, as a final preparation for a major assault.

FORMING UP

Once an LCA had been lowered from the davits of its landing ship for an exercise or an assault, its crew had to unhook it, which was difficult work on earlier vessels. The captain of *Glengyle* complained that his four-man crews could not do this alone, and he attached two extra men to each LCA for the purpose – they displaced two soldiers but would then go ashore to join a naval beach party. He did not, however, suggest training the soldiers to help with the disengaging.

After disengaging, the boat might have to wait until the rest of the flotilla was in the water and the craft were assembled in formation. There was no set drill by the time of the 'Husky' landings in 1943:

Some circled their ships, others circled each their own side of the ship, others left the ship and just kept head on to the sea till they were picked up by their guide. It is suggested that GLENGYLE'S drill where the weather side craft circle until formed up, then cross the bows and are joined by the lee side craft, which have been waiting alongside, seems a lot to recommend it in the rough weather experienced.

For tactical purposes the craft were divided into flights, which reflected army more than naval needs:

'Flight' is a term denoting a naval formation of landing craft, and it includes troops travelling in these craft. The landing craft will be organised in one or more flights, depending on the numbers available. A flight will generally contain a complete unit with any attached troops, and may be organised in waves to ensure that the unit lands in the correct tactical formation.[2]

Even when putting on a display for the King before the Normandy invasion, it was difficult to keep LCAs precisely in line.

Flights had different tasks. 'The duty of the first flight will usually be to capture and secure the landing place. ... The role of subsequent flights will be to pass through and secure the covering position or to support the first flight to the main objective.'

On the way to a landing it was better to keep craft in line ahead with one behind another. This presented a smaller target to the enemy, allowed them to use a narrow swept channel through a minefield and it was easier for the craft to keep station on one another. A standard flotilla of twelve boats would usually form up in two lines, with any support craft stationed to windward from where attack was most likely. Formation was deliberately kept loose, however, in case of aircraft attack. If that was a serious danger the craft might adopt the 'loose formation', with the boats arranged roughly in diamonds or diagonals. At night or in poor visibility the craft would be in close order, a boat's length apart in each column with the columns thirty yards apart. In daylight or under attack they would assume open order, fifty yards apart and with the columns seventy-five yards apart.

Some officers thought that formation-keeping was the most difficult part of the operation:

> The special problems connected with beaching the Landing Craft and with the management of the troops embarked, are popularly regarded as the main item in the training of Landing Craft crews. Actually however, they constitute the least difficult part of Naval Training. The average seaman can quickly be taught how to beach a Landing Craft and any officer of average power of command and common sense, can learn how to handle troops without difficulty. On the other hand the training needed to operate in company at sea is far and away the most difficult to provide. It calls for real experience in realistic conditions, which can only be provided by exercising in company in waters similar to those in which the force will have to operate.

TOWING

Occasionally, landing craft might be towed into action, as was the case in the attack on Elba in 1944. One major landing craft, such as an LCT, could tow two LCAs, one in each quarter. A motor launch could tow one LCA. A forty-foot rope was attached on each side of the LCA, with one end fixed to the after hoisting eye, then through an eye fitted under the bow. Together the ropes on each side formed a bridle and were shackled together forward of the bow and attached to the tow rope proper. This was recommended to be sixty feet long, although shortened considerably in heavy weather. If the bridle was properly adjusted there was no need for the craft to be steered, but the crew would remain on board to bail out water to take action in case the tow parted and to bring the craft alongside a parent ship at the loading point. The maximum speed of tow was twelve knots, eight knots was considered much safer and six knots was common in practice. Hedgerow craft behaved badly under tow because of the greater weight they carried – two were lost on the way to Sicily, and many more on the way to Normandy. On arrival at the lowering point, the tow was cast off and the LCAs came alongside the transports to take the troops on board.

SIGNALLING

Communication with and between LCAs during an assault was kept to a minimum. As the landing craft signal handbook of 1942 stated:

> It is the intention to provide Landing Craft with simple means of communication only, as trained communication ratings cannot be spared for these craft. If these communications are correctly and efficiently handled, the operational scope of these craft will be greatly increased. All operations should, however, be planned on simple lines and, if nothing untoward occurs, little signalling should be necessary.

Moreover, as the pamphlet emphasised, 'It is VITAL at all times, but more particularly so during the initial stages of the landing, that NOT ONE UNNECESSARY SIGNAL IS MADE … .'[3]

Means of signalling included torches, megaphones, radio sets and flags, each with its advantages and disadvantages. Torches in several colours were obviously for use at night, but they had to be screened to give the minimum acceptable amount of light, and could never be pointed in the direction of the enemy positions. They could flash Morse letters. Megaphones could be used to send any kind of message without the need for codes, but

Using flag signals to control the formation.

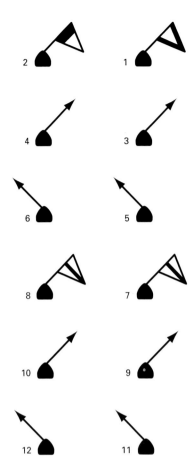

2 1

4 3

6 5

8 7

10 9

12 11

A loose formation recommended for use when there is a risk of air attack. The flags show the flotilla and group leaders.

obviously the range was limited, and might break the silence that was necessary for surprise. They were probably most useful when the flotillas were forming up.

Radio transmitters were normally allocated to sub-divisional leaders and above. The portable Type 66 set, also supplied to the army, used voice transmission over a range of about five miles over the water. It was used very sparingly so as to avoid giving the enemy notice that something was happening. Each boat carried a set of eight signal flags from the international code. The A flag held vertically instructed the group to form single line ahead, waved horizontally it meant, 'Form loose formation number two'. By day the A and Y flags held vertically ordered the flotilla to take up a formation as previously ordered, by night the letters A and Y were sent by blue or white light. The Y flag held vertically meant 'anchor', as did the flashing of Ys by blue or white light. There were code signs for squadron, divisional and sub-divisional leaders as well as navigational leaders and each type of craft had a code letter – the LCA's was A, the LCT's was T.

NAVIGATION

Clearly, good navigation was essential in any assault if the troops were to be landed on the right beaches in darkness or bad weather. According to the Director of Combined Training:

The chief problem with which they will have to contend is the pilotage one, of finding the right beach within 100 yards at the right time. To train an officer or a coxswain to do this with any success requires considerably more than three weeks, in view of the instruction in Beach Pilotage, and Navigational Aids, as well as ordinary Pilotage that is involved.[4]

This was not easy from an LCA, for it was difficult to fit even the simplest navigational aids. There was no room for a gyro compass, and magnetic compass was subject to a good deal of error, known as deviation, in a steel-plated hull. Selected craft, usually sub-divisional leaders, were fitted with steering compartments armoured in non-magnetic materials, but even that was not very satisfactory. Iron and steel were kept three feet from the compass, whereas in a normal warship these were usually kept at least ten feet away. Deviation might still vary considerably from day to day, and the presence of troops with the weapons and steel helmets made it worse. One extempore solution was to fit a compass centrally in the vessel away from the armour plate, on a 'bath board'. It was removed before the troops disembarked. Navigational plotting was impossible in the confined spaces of a normal LCA, and coxswains were not normally trained in it. There were plans to fit some LCSs with the Bigsworth board, a rather primitive chart table that had been developed by the RAF in the 1930s for use in two-seater aircraft.

Infrared guiding devices were tried early in the war, but these depended on the landing ship in which they were fitted being in exactly the right place to start with. Another method used was for a different craft, such as a motor launch (ML), to lead in the LCAs. The ML was not entirely suitable for this. It could not be carried in an LSI and had to meet the craft offshore – an arrangement that often went wrong. It was about three times as fast as a loaded LCA and was difficult to steer at low speeds. It made less leeway in a wind and as a result it might be difficult for the LCAs to follow its course. It had a draught of more than four feet so it could not go far inshore, and its wooden construction made it fragile. From November 1943, about forty American LCP(L)s were converted into Landing Craft, Navigation (LCN).

Otherwise, assault craft relied on visual identification of points on shore to find the right beach. Coxswains were issued with diagrams showing the salient features, perhaps prepared from photographs taken through the periscope of a submarine. It was relatively easy in mountainous country such as on Sicily, where there were plenty of cliffs and headlands to identify. It was much harder in the flatter lands of Normandy, especially if a preliminary bombardment might destroy features such as church steeples. Sergeant Frederick Turner was coxswain of one of the craft of the 556th Flotilla on Juno Beach in 1944, and was pleased to find that 'The buildings on the sea front at Bernieres appeared intact and a replica of the panoramic photographs we had been shown earlier.'[5]

BEACHING

On cruising or approaching a beach, the coxswain was at the helm and the stoker in the engine compartment. The bowman was right forward on the starboard side, the sternsheetman found a position between the seats aft on the port side. On close approach to the beach the craft would form into line abreast in the hope that each would touch down at exactly the same moment and the troops could disembark at the right places. Normally this was done by the leader stopping in the water, while the other craft took up prescribed speeds to come alongside him in the correct order. An alternative, if the craft were passing in line ahead along the shore, was for each craft to turn together when opposite the beach.

Most practitioners of amphibious warfare placed great store on the kedge anchor, which would be dropped from the stern just before a craft hit the beach. It would be used to haul the boat off again once the troops had disembarked, and in a cross wind or tide it would help keep the boat straight – the bows were aground, the stern was not and it might be swept into a precarious position parallel to the beach. But the kedge was not always used. The official instructions to minor landing craft crews suggested that it need not be deployed in the first wave of a surprise assault, because it would slow down things and reduce the advantage of surprise. Furthermore, as each man disembarked, the action of his feet on the ramp would tend to push the boat backwards, and of course it would be lightened after the men had left so there was little danger of grounding even if the tide was falling fast. While beaching in these conditions, the order 'stand by to beach' should be whispered. The bowman should feel the boat grounding and let the ramp tackle down quietly without any further order from the coxswain, and the doors should be opened at the last moment.

Often there was no chance to use the kedge, as was the case on some of the Normandy beaches that were too crowded with craft and debris to allow any space to drop an anchor. On Juno Beach in 1944, the captain of *Prince David* reported, 'There was quite a heavy swell and a strong current on our starboard quarter but due to the weaving approach it was impossible to use kedges.'6

But it was more normal to drop the kedge, especially if any surf was expected, and it had to be got ready during the final approach. On the order 'stand by to beach', the bowman got the tackle ready to let down the bow ramp, while the sternsheetman prepared the kedge and made sure it was free to run. The army platoon commander unbolted the armoured door and got ready to open it once the craft had beached. The order 'down kedge' was given about 120 feet or three boat's length from the water's edge and the sternsheetman let go. He eased it out until the craft hit the beach, when the bowman released the tackle to let down the ramp. The troops got out in their due order and the bowman went ashore on the windward side to secure a line on the beach. In surf two men might be necessary and one of the soldiers might be detailed to help. The soldiers should only disembark on orders from the coxswain who might wait for gaps between the waves. An extra man might be taken on if surf was expected, to help raise the kedge afterwards.

The kedge anchor and its gear was a source of weakness in many LCAs and accidents due to gear failure were frequent. During the Bruneval raid of 1942, Able Seaman John Thomas Bland was coxswain of *LCA 125* when the kedge line ran off the drum during beaching. He reversed his engine quickly to prevent the craft being wrecked and was decorated for his efforts. Another incident occurred during a small reconnaissance raid:

> The kedge of one of the craft parted under the jerking of an 'on shore' sea and the strain of hauling off. Instantly she was swung almost broadside on, and each succeeding wave bumped her further up the beach.
>
> One of her consorts came to her aid and circled as close as possible to her without coming inside the breakers (which would have landed her on the beach broadside on as well) and endeavoured to pass a line by throwing and wading. As the temperature was well below freezing and it was dark except for the illumination provided by the Hun's Verey lights these efforts were not successful and ended in two shuddering bodies being hauled aboard where their clothes up to their chests froze hard. Moreover it was already time for the covering force to withdraw so they must hurry.
>
> It was then that the officer of the floating L.C.A. evolved the plan of coming

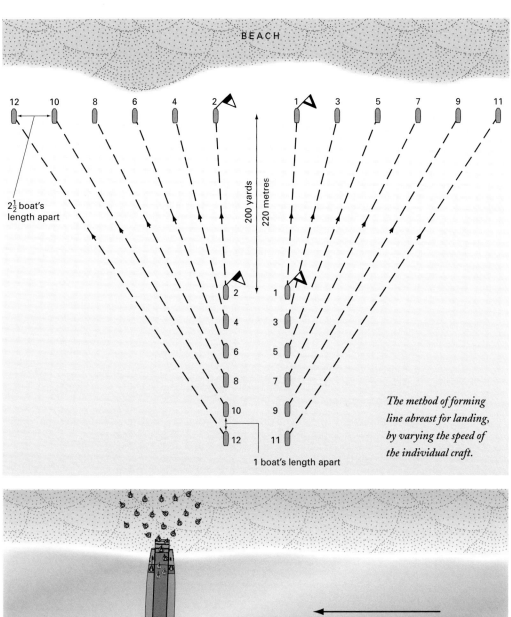

BEACH

12   10   8   6   4   2   1   3   5   7   9   11

$2\frac{1}{2}$ boat's
length apart

200 yards
220 metres

2   1
4   3
6   5
8   7
10   9
12   11

1 boat's length apart

*The method of forming
line abreast for landing,
by varying the speed of
the individual craft.*

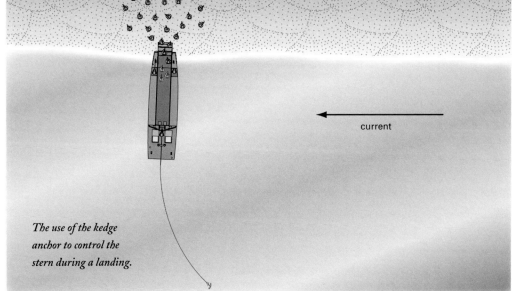

current

*The use of the kedge
anchor to control the
stern during a landing.*

straight bows on as near as possible to the counter of the grounded craft and a line was passed in this way. At first he tried to haul off with his own kedge but it came home. By backing and filling he managed to turn himself head out to sea and shift the point of tow from his bow to his counter. Going full ahead in this position he turned the grounded craft stern on to the sea, she rose a little on the next wave and in a moment was free. But he didn't stop towing till they were well out beyond the white line of breaking waves.[7]

Every coxswain was enjoined to keep the craft afloat at all times, but 'false beaches' were often encountered when reconnaissance was poor. If stuck on a sandbank, he should not use the engines in reverse at full power, because they might suck in debris and mud. Instead, the officers and crew should jump in and shove the boat off. Boathooks and poles were regarded as useless for this, and it was essential to get off quickly if the tide was falling

WITHDRAWING

While the use of the word 'assault' in its title implied an aggressive role, much of the LCA's early work was in picking up retreating armies. In many ways it was more difficult and dangerous than a landing. The enemy was probably alerted to the situation and his artillery and air power might do a great deal of damage. The troops taken off might well be demoralised and undisciplined and the LCA officer or coxswain would have to use his authority to stop it being overloaded. It was naturally harder to get a loaded craft off a beach than an unloaded craft and it could not be brought in too far. Commander Cassidi learned this early at Dunkirk in 1940:

> The beach proved to be exceptionally flat for a long distance off shore, and as the craft was carrying one week's provisions and an additional 200 gallons of petrol, she was drawing more water than usual. In view of this and the number of men it was intended to embark (50), it was necessary to drop the anchor on approaching the shore, and to hold the boat so that she was floating in about three feet of water. It was therefore necessary for the troops to wade some 50 yards when they were up to their waists in water, which entailed their being dragged bodily over the bow ramp which had previously been lowered.[8]

Although withdrawals were far less likely by 1943, the minor landing craft orders of that date gave details on how such an operation should be carried out. The coxswain should always be aware that a craft would sink three or four inches when fully loaded. He might decide not to use the kedge for the sake of speed, but if he did use it the anchor should be dropped as with a normal landing, but further out. When withdrawing, the coxswain should not use engine power until the kedge had been brought in – at least they had the advantage of being able to use troops to help haul in the anchor.

RETRACTING

Whether loaded with troops or not, a landing craft had to withdraw or 'retract' from the beach at some stage. Both seaman crew members would come forward to haul up the ramp, as silently as possible if surprise had been achieved. If the craft was not afloat, they would first push her off to avoid using engine power. They then would both go aft to haul in the anchor using a hand winch. Again the coxswain would use the engine as little as possible, both to keep up the element of surprise and to avoid damage. Once the kedge was in and the craft fully afloat, the engine might be put gently into astern and turned round to head out. This was a dangerous manoeuvre on a crowded beach and in Normandy more craft were damaged at this stage than any other:

> This flight appeared to have landed approximately ten minutes late but they managed to put their troops ashore in about 2 [feet] of water without much opposition. The unbeaching of this flight however was disastrous – largely, I consider, on account of the heavy congestion of craft which had occurred by this time, and the covering of beach obstacles owing to rising tide.
> No fewer than four craft of this flight were damaged by beach obstacles and subsequently sunk. A fifth craft was put out of action with a smashed rudder and broken steering wheel … .[9]

RETURNING TO THE SHIP

After the initial landing, the LCAs returned to the parent ship, or other ships as directed by the beachmasters or other officers, to carry out a ferry service until a port could be secured or built to replace them. As an officer in the LSI *Tegelberg* in 1944 put it, 'Once the assault is over, the hard work begins.' Relief crews were available at a rate varying between 15 and 50 per cent according to the nature of the operation so that they could take over from exhausted men. But in fact the craft often suffered worse than the crews during a landing.

Coming alongside a ship in bad weather was a hazard in itself, and one officer wrote after the North Africa landings:

> [We] always found when loading craft from a transport in a heavy swell, the coxswain's conning tower gets smashed in. Fenders are pretty well useless, and unless the craft are fitted with fenders after the manner of L.C.P. with additional fenders on each 'corner' and another on the conning tower, the hull will eventually require a long refit.

Some ships had ports in the sides where men could disembark, but this was not easy in the case of an LCA which was bobbing about in the sea. Troops might come down by scrambling net, but that was often painfully slow, and might take forty minutes per craft. On other occasions it might get out of hand and the same officer advised:

LCAs returning to Empire Halberd *after landing their troops during an exercise in May 1944.*

Beware of scrambling nets. Troops coming down nets with 60 lbs of equipment on their backs love to let go and fall into the boat below. It is because of the excitement I suppose. They always seem to land safely on their backs, the fall being broken by the equipment, but it is hell for anyone standing underneath them.[10]

It was difficult to hoist an LCA back on board without causing damage to the craft or its davit, but on the whole that was the preferred method of taking on men. Off Normandy, the captain of *Glenroy* complained, 'The conditions for hoisting were very bad indeed, and it says a good deal for the Marine Boats Crews that all Boats were successfully got on board with no damage to ship's gear, slight damage to boats, and one broken jaw!' Another captain went further: 'I must confess the prospect of hoisting any craft in the existing weather conditions frightened me a good deal more than the worst the enemy could have produced.'

6

THE ARMY ON BOARD

THE INFANTRY REGIMENT

The LCA was specifically designed to land infantry, perhaps the most underrated troops in the war. Major-General Utterson-Kelso believed that 'Infantry is the principal arm. It bears the main weight of battle. It suffers the heaviest casualties. All other arms support it.' This proved to be true in Combined Operations at least, but it did not prevent the other generals neglecting it, as Utterson-Kelso complained, the infantry was regarded as 'the legitimate dumping ground for the lowest form of military life'.[1] Infantrymen were often conscripts who offered no special skills or abilities and were not needed by the navy, the air force or the more technical branches of the army. What saved the force from demoralisation and neglect was its regimental tradition. The British infantry consisted of five regiments of foot guards and sixty-four more of line infantry. Each regiment was a training and administrative unit that never fought together. Instead it produced several battalions, two regular and perhaps three reserve units in peacetime, and up to a dozen in war. These would join battalions from other regiments to form brigades and divisions, which were the real fighting units.

Every regiment had an honorary colonel-in-chief, usually with strong royal, aristocratic or military connections. It had its own history, traditions, cap badge, nickname and uniform details. Its regimental colours were no longer carried into battle as they had been a century or so previously, but they were now displayed in a local church or museum; they bore a long list of battle honours – the combats in which the regiment had been involved over the centuries. It had a local base for recruitment and training and it was often revered there, particularly in country districts and in Scotland. Recruits might be attracted to the local regiment because of that, ignoring the superficially more attractive life and greater prestige to be found in other units or arms of service. When they joined they were indoctrinated in regimental tradition and history, and soon came to believe they were part of the finest body of fighting men in the world. The traditions were often transferred to Canada, whose regiments took part in the disastrous Dieppe raid and stormed Juno Beach during the Normandy invasion.

The Green Howards, which provided battalions for the Sicily, Anzio and Normandy landings, were first raised in 1688 as the 19th Regiment of Foot. The regiment had green facings, the colour of the collar and cuffs of its scarlet uniform and in 1744 it was commanded by a Colonel Howard and served in Flanders alongside the 3rd Regiment of Foot also commanded by a Howard. The 3rd Foot became the famous Buffs, the 19th gained the nickname of 'The Green Howards', which stuck and was adopted as the official title in 1921. It was based at Richmond in Yorkshire and its colonel-in-chief was the exiled King Haakon of Norway. It had raised twenty-four battalions in the First World War and won twelve Victoria Crosses. It would raise eleven in this war, of which six saw highly active service and three took part in amphibious operations.

A battalion was commanded by a lieutenant-colonel. By 1943, it consisted of four companies of 126 officers and men each, and a headquarters that also included heavy weapons and transport and had a total of 256 officers and men. With a total of thirty-three officers, thirty-six senior NCOs and 717 men of the rank of corporal and below, it could be carried conveniently in one of the *Glen* ships, along with about 170 specialists such as engineers and signallers.

Some battalions became, in effect, specialists in amphibious warfare. The 2nd Battalion of the Devonshire Regiment landed in LCAs with the first waves in Sicily and Normandy. The 1st Battalion of the Green Howards landed in Sicily and at Anzio, while the 6th and 7th Battalions were both evacuated from Dunkirk and then fought in the desert war. They were under Montgomery at Alamein and helped pursue the Germans and Italians out of North Africa. They went back to Egypt for amphibious warfare training at Kabret and took part in the landings on Sicily. Both sailed back to Britain in October 1943 and began normal infantry training with a view to landing in France three days behind the first wave. But, in February 1944, Montgomery decided to place his more experienced regiments in the lead role and the two went back to amphibious warfare training, including two weeks at Inveraray. They were to form part of the 50th Division, which was to land on Gold Beach, where Company Sergeant-Major Stanley Hollis won the only Victoria Cross of that day.

Battalion commanders often played a role in planning the operation and the certainly needed to be briefed in detail.

> The assault battalion commander, when receiving orders regarding the beaches for the landing, will be given all available intelligence regarding the beaches or landing places and the enemy's dispositions in the area in which the unit is to land; he will also require tome of high and low water, sun and moon rise and set, and degree of moonlight to be expected. The troops placed under his command will normally travel in the same ship as the battalion.[2]

The platoon

The LCA was specifically designed to carry an infantry platoon of thirty-one troops, a sub-division of a company and the smallest unit normally commanded by a commissioned officer – although at the beginning of the war there was a plan to have a proportion of these commanded by warrant officers. Apart from that, a platoon commander was normally a lieutenant or second lieutenant, with a

Men of the 6th Battalion, Green Howards, training for the Normandy invasion.

sergeant as second-in-command. Its headquarters under the officer consisted of the sergeant, a runner and batman who might also carry a radio. There was also three-man section under a lance corporal who operated a 2in mortar, and sometimes a PIAT (projector, infantry, anti-tank) rifle was also carried.

The rest of the platoon was made up of three sections, each headed by a corporal. At the beginning of the war a section had eight men, by 1943 that had been increased to ten, and so the total number in the platoon was now thirty-seven. The naval authorities resisted any increase in the number to be carried in an LCA, and in most assaults engineers and signallers still had to be carried in addition, so platoons were not always at full strength when they landed on a beach.

It will be noted that platoons are allowed at a strength of 30 each; this is dependent on the dimensions of the landing craft. The five additional places in the craft are required for the personnel of other arms who have to land at the same time as the assaulting platoon. The allotment of these personnel to craft can only be made after deciding the immediate requirements on shore.[3]

The corporal in charge of each section was usually armed with a Sten sub-machine gun, but its main weapon was the Bren light machine gun, operated by a squad of three under the lance-corporal who was also second in command of the section. According to a training pamphlet:

The light machine gun is the principal weapon of the infantry and, except in cases where the need for extreme mobility outweighs the need for fire power, it should always be carried by sections in action. *All ranks must be experts in its use.*[4]

The rest of the section carried the Lee-Enfield .303in bolt action rifle, the most common weapon of the British infantry since the beginning of the century. As well as ammunition for his own rifle, each member of the section carried several of the Bren gun's characteristic curved magazines. A platoon was quite a sophisticated combat unit by 1940, with several types of weapon – an officer's pistol for self defence, three Brens, twenty-nine rifles, four Stens, a mortar and a number of hand grenades distributed among the men.

Platoons were combined into companies, and in the early stages it was planned that the standard group of three LCAs would land one company. Obviously some would have to be left behind, as a company totalled 126 officers and men while three LCAs could take a maximum of 105, and probably less on most operations. By the time of the invasion of Normandy, five LCAs were allocated to each company, which also included a number of assault engineers. This kept the army organisation intact but it did not necessarily conform to the structure of the naval flotilla. For example, ten LCAs of the 536th Flotilla from *Glenearn* landed A and C companies of the 2nd Battalion, the East Yorkshire Regiment on the Queen Red sector of Sword Beach, while a similar number of LCAs of the 535th Flotilla from *Empire Cutlass* landed A and C companies of the 1st Battalion the South Lancashire Regiment. Both flotillas would then return to their parent ships to pick up the rest of the battalions.

SPECIALISTS

Engineers were often landed with the assault infantry, especially if the beach was heavily defended or they expected to stay. In *Glengyle* in 1942, *ALC No 8* was to carry a Royal Engineers party of ten, along with fifteen officers and men of the infantry battalion headquarters and ten signallers. *ALC No 10* carried twenty-one sappers who would do the heavier engineering work, plus the rest of the headquarters. In the standard loading arrangement of 1942, it was common for each LCA to carry an engineer detachment of four or five men, and leave out an equivalent number from the infantry platoon. The engineers would sit near the bows and be ready to disembark quickly just behind the platoon commander in order to deal with obstacles and enemy defences. Any heavy engineering equipment would come in larger vessels such as LCTs. The engineers in the LCAs with the assaulting infantry carried hand equipment including wire cutters, axes, picks, shovels, and explosives and detonators of various types. Sometimes they had Bangalore torpedoes – extendable tubes with explosives at one end – that could be used to detonate barbed wire and other obstacles. They took up no more space in an LCA than standard infantry equipment such as mortars and machine guns. For the Normandy invasion, one flight from *Glenearn* carried two companies of the East Yorkshire Regiment, plus two detachments of the 264th Field Company of the Royal Engineers, a unit of Royal Navy Beach Commandos, and a Landing Craft Obstruction Clearance Unit. In other cases, special craft were designed to fulfil various roles.

In a large scale invasion, it was risky to concentrate too many specialists of the same kind in a single craft, because it might be lost. One solution, as used in June 1944, was for the craft carrying specialists and headquarters units to alternate with those carrying the infantry platoons. The 1st Battalion the South Lancashire Regiment was taken out in its LSI and ten LCAs were planned to land the first wave precisely at H-hour. The starboard end of the landing was to be marked by an LCA carrying thirty men from one platoon of A Company, plus four others including part of the naval beach party. Alongside was *LCA 118* with a total of fifteen men, including the commander of A Company with a sniper, two runners, two stretcher bearers, an interpreter, two signallers, a regimental policeman and five pioneers for clearing obstacles. The rest of the space was taken up by pioneer and medical stores and wireless sets. The next craft carried thirty-three men of another platoon of A Company, then *LCA 120* had the rest of the company HQ, including the sergeant-major, a sniper, a runner, four stretcher bearers, three signallers and five men from the Royal Engineers forming part of an assault demolition team. Another LCA carried the remaining platoon of A Company, and the order was similar in the next five in the line, carrying C Company and its support – *LCA 126* also carried part of the naval beach party and was to mark the other end of the landing area.

The second wave included B and D companies and was to land twenty minutes later in another ten LCAs, this time with three craft carrying headquarters and specialists, and more crammed with personnel. *LCA 149*, third from starboard, had fourteen infantry officers and men, nearly all the headquarters of B Company. It also had eight field engineers forming parts of assault demolition and mine clearance teams, four artillerymen to set up a forward observation post, two men form an anti-tank reconnaissance party and the regimental padre. *LCA 154*, sixth in line, carried similar party for D Company. *LCA 156* carried the battalion headquarters, twenty-seven officers and men including the commanding officer, intelligence, signalling and pioneer officers as well as signallers, clerks, policemen, pioneers, the CO's batman and small groups from the Royal Engineers and the Royal Artillery. *LCA 155* had the reserve battalion headquarters, with the second in command, adjutant, regimental sergeant major and another complement of specialists. The third wave, including most of the battalion's vehicles, would land twenty-five minutes later in LCTs.

SOLDIERS' EQUIPMENT

The members of an infantry platoon, like nearly all British soldiers during the war, wore the khaki battledress uniform with its short jacket in temperate climate, and a lighter uniform, known as khaki drill, in the Mediterranean and other warm theatres. They wore gaiters made of webbing or canvas, with belts, shoulder straps and ammunition pouches in the same material. Each soldier carried a considerable weight, which was around ninety pounds at the time of the Normandy invasion. A basic rifleman had to carry one hundred rounds of ammunition in addition to two Bren magazines with twenty-eight rounds each, and usually a hand grenade. A special mess tin was provided for combined operations, to help a man survive for up to forty-eight hours without replenishment. In addition, the soldier carried a water bottle, bayonet, waterproof cape and sometimes a gas mask, an entrenching tool and perhaps a pick or shovel as well. He was top-heavy and found it difficult to move on a ship or boat. This was not helped by his hob-nailed 'ammunition' boots, which were designed to cope with mud and sand rather than the slippery conditions on deck.

According to the instructions to infantry:

> The nature of the operation will usually require the troops to be 'self-contained' for 48 hours. Special mess tin rations for this period have been produced and will be carried on the man in addition to the emergency ration. It is important that the men carrying out the initial assault be lightly equipped. There is little room to spare in a crowded LCA carrying a rifle platoon and men must have their hands as free as possible if they are to clear the craft quickly and get over the beaches. ...
>
> Climatic conditions will dictate whether greatcoats can be dispensed with for two or three days until the bulk of the transport arrives. If required they will have to be taken ashore in bundles during the ferry service and be dumped in the assembly area for forwarding when transport can be made available.
>
> In certain circumstances it has been found preferable for each man to land with one blanket rolled in bandolier or strapped on the haversack or small pack; alternatively, they may wear leather jerkins which allow free movement.[4]

Going into action, a rifle company would carry:

> Personal equipment, arms, Bren guns (less tripods). [Anti-tank] rifle, 2-inch mortars and [ammunition], Verey pistols.
>
> Personnel of the first flight not landing in initial assault carry additional tools. Personnel in ferry service may manhandle box [ammunition] for [battalion] res[erve], tools and greatcoats to [battalion] assembly area.[5]

Men were issued with inflatable life vests, which were worn round the chest and supported by straps over the shoulders. They were inflated by mouth, and as a result of this each had to be at least partly inflated if the man was to stand any chance in the water. It was worn under the web equipment, which had to be ditched quickly if the man fell in. They were far less efficient than the 'Mae West' issued to the RAF and they would not keep an unconscious man's head above the water, although they were often known loosely as Mae Wests. Lance-Corporal Rolph Jackson's platoon met strong opposition on Juno Beach. 'We were still in the water when the section was cut down. Most of us had deflated the Mae Wests we were wearing, and possibly those that died had drowned'. Major A R C Mott had a more fortunate experience with his:

Down went the ramp and I jumped, no doubt starting to shout 'Get up them beaches' as ordered. This ended in bubbles, for the water was about seven feet deep. My Mae West saved me and brought me to the surface, with the LCA about to pass over me. I caught hold of a chain and was towed ashore.[6]

TRAINING

Battalions that were expected to take part in amphibious operations usually had intensive training with landing craft, sometimes at Inveraray and other home bases, and sometimes at Kabrit in Egypt, where they disembarked from concrete landing craft erected in the sands. A standard ten-day course for an infantry battalion began with a lecture and film on combined operations followed by practice in mock-up LCAs and other craft. The second day was spent in practising platoons and companies in moving 500 yards inland through beach obstacles and so on. Next day, they were given a demonstration, using models, of beach organisation and the duties of the landing officers and spent the rest of the time on trucks used as mock-up landing craft. On the fourth day, they had a demonstration on waterproofing vehicles and lectures on signals and life on board ship, followed by practice on climbing down ladders in the dark, into the shape of an LCA that was marked out by tape on a parade ground, quarry or gym. The programme would conclude with a full-scale

Lord Mountbatten (on the right) watches an exercise at Dundonald Camp in Scotland. Troops land from a mock LCA, passing through a pool of water on the way.

exercise in which '... a fully developed scale of beach defences should be employed; mock up craft and all available means of destruction of obstacles should be used. A controlled enemy is also advisable.'[7]

The 2nd Battalion of the East Lancashire Regiment did intensive training at Inveraray in 1941, learning to land from LCAs, to seize an immediate objective, to develop a beachhead and advance rapidly inland to the main objective. They were inspected successively by the Prime Minister and Field Marshall Sir John Dill, the Colonel of the Regiment. They moved to Scapa Flow for more exercises and were inspected by the King, then to inland Galashiels for yet more training. In March 1942, they were suddenly called out and embarked on two LSIs at Glasgow. Once at sea, they were told that their objective was the island of Madagascar.

Away from the main Combined Operations bases, infantry regiments were encouraged to organise their own training. One method was to construct mock-up craft out of wood, brick or concrete, and in the case of an LCA the main points to note were the overhead cover down the sides of the craft, and the ramp, which if possible should be constructed over a pool of water. Another possibility was to exercise using trucks in place of the landing craft. An LCA could be represented by a three-ton lorry with its hood removed, and able to accommodate thirty-five men. During the exercise each 'craft' would be 'preceded by a bicyclist carrying a flag of a distinctive colour and lettered to show its type'. Umpires would observe the turn round of each craft, and 'impose the necessary delays to make timings conform to actual operations'.

The 6th and 7th Battalions of the Green Howards formed part of the 50th Division which had already fought in North Africa and Italy. When they disembarked in Britain in November 1943, it was assumed that they would form part of one of the later waves for the invasion of France, but in February 1944 they were upgraded to the first wave because of their experience. They were sent to Inveraray for two weeks of Combined Operations training, and then to camps in southern England until they embarked in landing ships on 1 June.

The 2nd Battalion, the Devonshire Regiment had its first amphibious training from mock landing craft at Mena in the shadow of the Pyramids, and used it in the invasion of Sicily. At Inveraray in March 1944, they were surprised how much they still had to learn to take part in a much larger-scale operation. They too moved to the south of England and were pleased to be put on board *Glenroy,* in which they had trained. They did more exercises in Studland Bay and on Hayling Island, sometimes as part of a full division.

PREPARATIONS FOR LANDING

A landing craft had to be 'tactically loaded', so that everything was available in the right order.

> The greatest care must be taken in the stowage of ships of the assaulting force. Mistakes once made cannot be rectified afterwards. The rule 'last in first out' must be strictly

adhered to and the stowage of tanks, guns, transport stores, etc., must be strictly in accordance with the tactical requirements of the landing.[8]

This was less of a problem with LCAs, which usually carried men rather than stores and were not expected to take long to unload in any case.

As the landing ship approached the area to be attacked, the troops were given a meal an hour before they were due to stand to. As soon as it was finished, in the case of a night operation, white lights were replaced with red to accustom their eyes to the dark. The troops were issued with rations for the attack, with a view to making each self-sufficient for forty-eight hours if necessary. There was a double issue of the 'standard ration' consisting of dehydrated meat, tea and oatmeal, plus biscuits, sweets and chocolate. If the sea voyage in the LCA was relatively long, the men might also be issued with tins of 'self-heating' soup which could be lit by a match or cigarette and would come to the boil in four minutes. Emergency rations were also carried, only to be opened on the orders of an officer if other means of supply failed, but it was hoped that the men would be replenished by the normal organisation long before that was necessary.

Soldiers in the first wave of a landing usually embarked in the LCAs while they were suspended from the side of the LSI and were understandably wary during the process. Since not all LSIs were fully converted, there might be a gap of up to three feet between the ship and the boat, which was disturbing to a fully loaded infantryman in the dark and in heaving seas. A naval officer gave advice on how to handle it.

> The first thing upon which everybody remarks with horror is the width of the gap between the ship's side and the perilously swinging boat, although you have a bowsing in tackle doing its best at either end. Try and comfort them, but do not bring the boat into the ship's side with slip wires, it interferes with the lowering and makes your ultimate get-away so slow.
>
> Even if it is pitch dark, blowing half a gale, and frightfully cold, the bridging of this gap can be achieved quite simply, and without the loss of (m)any soldiers if you carry out a simple drill.
>
> One sailor should stand on the gunwale and take each soldier's weapon, he then passes it down to his chum standing in the well of the boat. The sailor on the gunwale then emits soft alluring cries of encouragement to the terrified soldier, and should catch him as he jumps across. The soldier then walks aft, having both hands free (although he may not know quite what to do with them), climbs down the small ladder by the engine-room door, into the well of the boat where he breathes a heavy sigh of relief, is handed back his weapon, and sits down in his right place.[9]

Standard systems were devised for seating the men on the three benches on board an LCA, and embarkation was always done in reverse order. When it was complete with an infantry platoon, the officer stood near the bows, ready to lead his men out, with the runner and batman just behind him. One of the Bren gunners operated his weapon in the port cockpit. Number 1 section sat on the

Troops entering an LCA, which has been lowered for the purpose. Another one is seen at higher level to the right. Drawn by Edward Ardizzone during the Sicily invasion.

centre bench, with its leader just behind the command group. Numbers 2 and 3 sections sat on either side, with the platoon sergeant and the mortar group towards the rear. Orders demanded that the men should sit astride the benches ready to disembark, but after the Sicily invasion it was suggested that if they were carrying large packs, those on the outer benches should sit facing inwards to allow room for the pack. Photographs show many variations, and the men in the centre might want to talk to their friends on one side or the other.

There were variations when more mixed units were carried, as Jim Wilkins of the Queen's Own Rifles of Canada describes:

At about 4:30 we were ordered to go on deck where sailor guides took us to our appointed stations. Our landing craft were at deck level and we could just climb in. The first section was No 1 of B Company on the port side. They sat facing in. The next group was on the starboard side consisting of odds and sods; our platoon sergeant, Freddy Harris, who had given up a commission to be with us; the company sergeant-major Bill Wallace; company staff such as runners and stretcher bearers; and combat

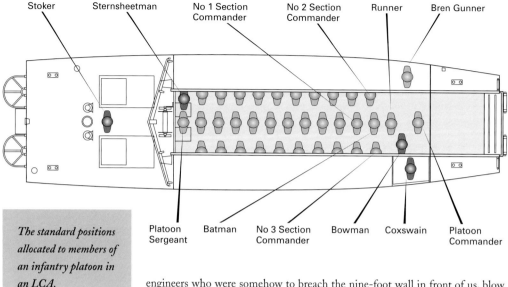

The standard positions allocated to members of an infantry platoon in an LCA.

engineers who were somehow to breach the nine-foot wall in front of us, blow up pillboxes and gun positions. Next, came my section – No 2 of B Company. We climbed in and sat on a low bench running down the centre facing forward. I was at the very back.[10]

The craft was then lowered into the water amid great tension.

As we were lowered away, no word was passed between those still on the ship and the first flight in the tossing LCA. The moment was too big, perhaps. Maybe they too wondered what it would be like when we touched down. This was to be my first action, in which there would be a sudden transition from comparative peace to war. In front of us the beach was hardly distinguishable in the smoke and dust, but before we could study it we were crouched in the bottom of the craft for the last lap.[11]

On board the LCA, the coxswain was in command while the vessel was afloat, even though he might only be an able seaman, equivalent to an army private, and his passengers were led by an officer. He often had to assert himself to prevent his craft being overloaded, or the men standing up at the wrong moment or making too much noise.

SEASICKNESS

Bulldozer, the magazine of Combined Operations, told the sailors that, 'On an operation the soldiers have a great ordeal before them, including seasickness.' It was not unknown in bigger ships such as LSI(L)s. On the way around Africa towards Egypt in February 1941, the three *Glen*s hit force 8 to 9 gales and most of the troops, not to mention half of the ship's company, were very sick indeed. But on the whole it was much rarer on larger ships. The short length of the LCA made it vulnerable in quite average sea conditions, its flat bottom and shallow draught caused it to react to every wave and it often had to face surf as it approached the beach. It could be quite a shock when the men first entered it:

> We climbed down the side of our troop ship on rope ladders and into LCAs. These small craft bobbed about as the skipper of each craft tried to head for the shore. One moment, we were down at the bottom of a wave which was so deep that as we looked up, all we could see was sky. The next moment, we were on the top of these huge waves, looking down.[12]

A study showed that seasickness was worst in an LCA after thirty-five to forty-five minutes in rough seas. There was little sickness during the first fifteen minutes, and few new cases after ninety minutes. But the average voyage from the lowering point seven miles offshore took at least one hour, and probably rather more allowing time for forming up and delays in rough seas. This was precisely the time in which the men would be at their worst. Men seated aft in the vessel were less vulnerable and it was recommended that key personnel be seated there, but of course not platoon commanders. Drugs were used, but were not totally effective. The simpler remedies, such as eyeing the horizon or lying flat, were not available in a crowded craft. Doctors suggested that men might be allowed to stand up for ten minutes after vomiting, but that was not easy to arrange in cases of mass sickness, or under fire. Sweets and biscuits should be issued, at least five vomit bags should be supplied to each man and ground sheets should be available to keep them warm. But in the Normandy landings one Canadian soldier found, 'We were so sick that we had preferred to be shot on the beaches rather than go back on those landing craft.'[13] Fortunately, victims usually recovered very quickly from seasickness as soon as they got on shore, and most troops were soon fighting fit after landing

APPROACHING THE BEACH

Most of the soldiers were passive during the tense run in to the beach, but there were opportunities for some to take part in the action. The three Bren gunners might be employed, one on each side to fire on the beaches and a third in the centre to fire at enemy aircraft. Marine Breen used his weapon on the way to Dieppe in 1942, claiming to have knocked out an enemy position in a casino. But sometimes it was suggested that they should not fire the Brens unless they had a specific target, because they only drew attention to themselves. It was possible to fire 2in or 3in mortars from platforms aft in the boat, although it needed fitting and special training and troops were warned not to use too high a trajectory, because the bomb would come down on their own craft.

Otherwise, the troops tried to keep calm as they approached the greatest test of their lives. On the run in to Sword Beach in June 1944, the men in *LCA 796* played cards and ate the meals which had been issued to them. *ML 202* played gramophone records such as *Roll out the Barrel* as she guided LCAs into Sword Beach, while a battalion bugler on board one of them sounded out 'Cookhouse'.

Meanwhile, 'Other craft cheered themselves against the prevailing nausea by community singing and by a mariner's "brew-up", in the shape of tea issued from the hot containers embarked in these craft.' None of this could have helped to achieve tactical surprise.

The craft did not always beach in shallow water. According to Sergeant Mackenzie of the Royal Engineers:

> We kidded ourselves that as we were on an LCA, we would land straight on the beach without getting our feet wet. At about 100 yards from the beach, the bloke in charge of the LCA called out, 'Sorry, lads, this is the best I can do. Mind how you go off the ramp as it might crush your feet.' Well off we went: bed roll on shoulder, kit on back, rifle slung round neck, and fingers crossed.[14]

On beaching, the platoon commander unbolted the bow doors. He would land first, followed by his batman and runner, and then No 1 section seated down the centre, and Nos 2 and 3 sections, down the sides. They were followed by the platoon sergeant and the mortar men. The whole unit was expected to disembark within nine seconds, but this might not be achieved if there was heavy surf and the craft was pounding, or there was a large amount of seasickness.

Some of the men from the LSI *Princess Maud* took some time to get moving from the LCAs on the morning of 6 June, but in general they were expected to move fast.

> It is most important that assault craft shall be cleared quickly. However, if there is wire on the beaches, it may in certain circumstances be preferable for men to remain in the craft while individuals, who must be detailed in advance, go forward to breach the wire.
>
> As soon as the troops have landed from craft they must get forward inland as quickly as possible; on no account must they remain on or near the beaches. If troops or carriers are landed on the wrong beach where a unit other than their own has landed, they should at once place themselves under the orders of the latter unit and work inland with it until the situation allows of their rejoining their own unit.[15]

The moment of disembarkation and the crossing of the beach were the most dangerous periods, and in Normandy it was the point where most of the enemy defenders opened fire for the first time. One LCT sailor returning from the first flight on Sword Beach shouted to the first group of LCAs, 'It's a piece of cake'. But the enemy was now awake.

> Shortly afterwards, however, the Hun began to come to life. Mortar and rifle fire from snipers began to take their toll, and did so increasingly as the beaches became cluttered with stranded craft and vehicles drowned by the rising tide. But to soldiers and sailors alike, the vast majority of them under fire for the first time in their lives, if they ceased to joke, it was because this was more as they had visualised an Assault to be and they only drove on the harder.[16]

When a company of the Regina Rifles landed on Juno Beach in five LCAs, each craft reported one by one:

> All troops gone clear of the water, then three were seen to fall when running up the beach.
>
> Two were hit as soon as they attempted to leave the craft. The remainder of the troops sustained a few casualties when running up the beach.
>
> Six were seen to fall whilst running up the beach.
>
> A number seen to be hit when crossing the sand.
>
> A few casualties amongst the troops once they were seen to be clear of the water.[17]

Life was rarely pleasant for soldiers in an LCA. They were crammed in tightly with little view of what was going on, with only thin armour and unit comradeship to comfort them. Often they were chronically seasick, which could only be ended by disembarkation, with the possibility of sudden and violent death or injury. It was no better for the officers, who found themselves under the control of coxswains and flotilla officers who were usually junior in rank and did not always give the impression that they knew what they were doing. Assuming they survived this, the soldiers went on to engage the beach defences and then move inland as fast as possible. They might be just at the beginning of a long campaign.

Specialist Craft and Roles

The assault landing craft was designed with the infantry in mind, although it had to be able to work with the other arms of the service to take a full part in any operation. It had comparatively little to do with armoured or transport units, because it was not designed to carry any kind of vehicle, except the bicycle and the handcart – in May 1940 the Inter-Service Training and Development Centre (ISTDC) paid £15 for a suitable handcart to carry heavier equipment ashore and in 1942 the loading tables for *Glenearn* showed a bicycle in nearly every LCA. The standard ordnance handcart had a total length of seven feet two inches including its pole, and was two feet nine inches wide so it could easily get out of the four feet six inches doors of an ALC. In addition, the basic ALC design helped fulfil the role of several other branches of the army, including the artillery and the engineers.

The support landing craft

The support landing craft was conceived by the ISTDC in 1938 at the same time as the LCA, and it used the same hull. It too was designed to be carried on board a Landing Ship, Infantry, and be lowered from its davits. It was intended to give close-range covering fire to a landing, so it was fitted with two 0.5in machine guns, a heavier calibre than was normally carried by the infantry. They were simply mounted on tubular posts in the troop well, staggered on either side of the hull and the gunners had to rely on the boat's armour for protection. The steering

A support landing craft Mark 1.

The Mark 2 version, with heavier armament in a turret.

shelter was placed aft in the well so that it interrupted the field of fire as little as possible. The bow doors and ramp no longer needed to open, but their shape remained unchanged from the ALC. The anchor and its gear could now be fitted forward, as there was no need to kedge off a beach. The biggest problem was the 4in smoke mortar, which was fitted forward in the bows just aft of the armour plate. There was no suitable projectile which could alight on either water or land and send up a cloud of smoke. The Board of Ordnance was too busy to give it attention and as a result Maund and his colleagues turned to the Gas School at Porton, which produced a bomb to be tested against the best that the Ordnance Board could do. The success of the Porton bomb, which 'sat up in the water or lay on the ground and made a magnificent smoke cloud' inspired the Ordnance Board to co-operate more. Normally one support landing craft was carried in the LSI at the rate of one per twelve-boat flotilla, replacing one of the ALCs. The first version became known as the Landing Craft, Support (LCS) Mark 1. Two were ordered with the first sixteen LCAs in November 1939 and eight were in service by June 1940.

In autumn 1941, the craft was redesigned to create the Mark 2, to be known as the Landing Craft, Support (Medium) Mark 2. The hull stayed the same, but the wheelhouse was moved slightly and an armoured turret containing the two 0.5in guns was fitted where it had been. The smoke projector moved slightly aft to just forward of midships, and the forward section was covered in except for a well for operating the anchor. Weight was increased from nine tons to twelve and a half tons because of the extra armour, but that only paralleled the rise in the ALC and was still within the scope of the LSI's strengthened davits. In all, thirty Mark 1s and 2s were built, but it was becoming clear that the landing craft bow was not really needed, though the shallow draft could be very useful. Thornycroft redesigned the hull in spring 1942. The afterpart remained generally similar, with square transom stern, propellers partly recessed in tunnels, almost flat bottom and

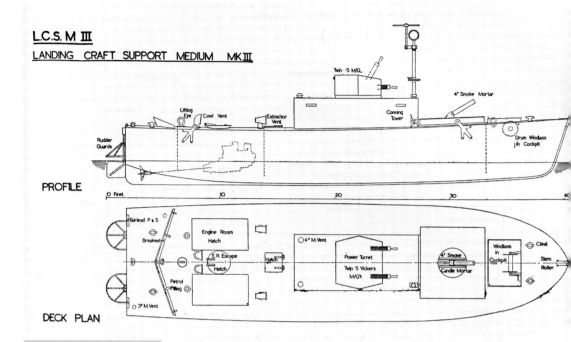

L.C.S. M III
LANDING CRAFT SUPPORT MEDIUM MK III

Twin ·5 M/G.

4" Smoke Mortar

Lifting Eye   Cowl Vent   Extractor Vent   Conning Tower

Rudder Guards

Drum Windlass in Cockpit

PROFILE

0 Feet   10   20   30   40

Fairlead P & S

Breakwater

Engine Room Hatch

E.R. Escape   Hatch   Hatch

Petrol Filling

3" M Vent

O 4" M Vent

Power Turret
Twin ·5 Vickers M/Gs

4" Smoke Candle Mortar

Windlass in Cockpit   Cleat   Stem Roller

DECK PLAN

almost vertical sides. The gun turret moved forward to midships to help balance the vessel, and the wheelhouse was now integral to the armoured structure under the guns. The smoke projector moved further forward, just aft of the anchor well in the bows, which were completely redesigned. The graceful 'sampan style' curve as seen from the side disappeared, and the two sides met to produce a much more conventional shape, with a 'hard chine' or sharp corners below to aid the transition to the square hull aft. The Landing Craft, Support (Medium) Mark 3 became the most common version. It was still recognisably a cousin of the LCA.[1]

The next stage was to produce a craft which could engage with enemy tanks. The Landing Craft, Support (Large) Mark 1 was also produced by Thornycroft but was six feet longer than a medium craft, weighed nearly twenty-five tons and was designed to be hoisted from derricks rather than davits, on the same basis as LCMs. It was not ready until April 1943, by which time its 2-pounder gun was outclassed as a tank weapon. The idea of a shipborne support craft had gone beyond its limits and future vessels of this type would be shore-to-shore craft, mostly based on the landing craft tank hull. As the landing craft flak, it could carry heavy or medium anti aircraft guns, and as the landing craft gun it might be fitted with 4.7in guns as in a modern destroyers, 25-pounder field guns as used by the army, or rapid fire 20mm Oerlikons. As the landing craft rocket, it could fire a devastating but very short salvo onto the beaches. The LCTs could also carry tanks or self-propelled artillery that was loaded so that it could fire on the beaches during the approach, before being landed to take part in the battle there.

This was only part of the great range of heavy support that became available as the war progressed. Naval gunfire had always been possible, from the 16in guns of a battleship with a shell weighing 2375 pounds, to the 4in guns of a corvette as used during the Lofoten Islands raid in 1941. Forward observation observers were landed to guide the fire, or they could be carried in LCG(M)s. Bombing was available in the form of heavy attacks to destroy the defences in advance of an attack, or fighter bombers launching rockets against tanks. But large ships could not come close inshore and their guns were relatively inaccurate – those of more than 6in calibre could not be used within 500 yards of one's own forces, and larger guns within 1000 yards. The landing forces still needed their own gunnery support, and the LCG(M) still had a role in that at the end of the war.

SMOKE SCREENS

The laying of a smoke screen was regarded as a primary function of the LCG(M) in its various forms, but it was little used in practice – an official handbook of June 1943 admitted that 'Knowledge of the use of smoke in Combined Operations, apart from area screening, is mainly theoretical ...'. During the Vaagsø raid in 1941 it was dropped by aircraft, but one bomb hit an LCA and caused about twenty casualties from burns. However, it was considered that the three bombs dropped accurately 'were of great value, for they enabled the troops

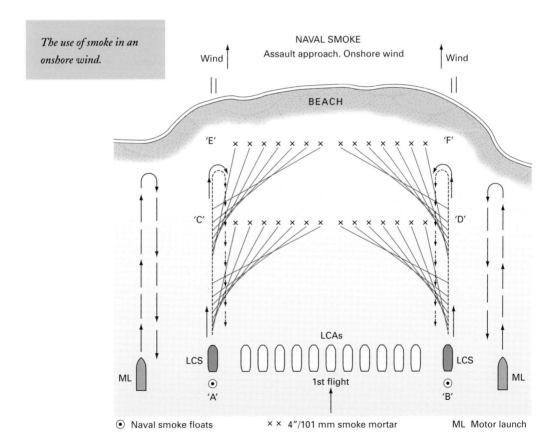

The use of smoke in an onshore wind.

to be put ashore with few casualties …'. Smoke was used to cover the withdrawal at Dieppe, but mostly it was laid by aircraft or LCMs.

The 1943 handbook envisaged three scenarios. If the wind was blowing onto the shore, two support craft would take up positions on the flanks of the landing craft and drop a float astern. They would then move ahead and use mortars to create two lines of smoke in front of the landing craft, so that it would be blown toward the beaches. It was hoped that the maximum amount would be on the beach just as the first wave touched down. In a cross wind, the support craft would also be on the flanks and would race ahead, firing diagonally upwind. An offshore wind could cause difficulty because the smoke might well blow onto the landing craft. The two support craft would fire it diagonally outwards towards the enemy positions to protect the flanks, but it was admitted that in these conditions, it might be better to use aircraft to lay the screen.[2]

SUPPORT CRAFT IN SERVICE

Otherwise, LCS(M)s saw service in many operations. Eight were at Dieppe, where it was intended that these, and the new landing craft flak, would give close support during the landings. *LCS 25* and *LCS 8*, for example, supported the unsuccessful attempt on the inner east flank at Puits, silencing enemy small-arms fire from point-blank range but proving ineffective against strengthened houses and pill boxes. *LCS 9* attempted to land the senior officer at Pourville but was sunk by gunfire. Six took part in the landings at Oran. *LCG(M) 29* was damaged when launched but *LCG(M) 31* from HMS *Royal Ulsterman* took her place and led a flotilla of ten boats carrying doctors and medical supplies to the beaches. At daylight it was hit but replied with its machine guns and smoke mortar and was able to return to its parent ship. During the landings in Sicily, they fired grapnels to help land American Rangers. At Salerno in 1943, *LCS 43* from *Prinses Astrid* was off Green Beach at daylight when she saw an enemy battery that was not engaged by any warships. She sailed in close and silenced it with her machine guns and mortar, and it was knocked out by the guns of a destroyer. Several craft, including *LCS 43*, then stayed on the beach for several days but became 'nobody's baby' as the crews had to scrounge for food and stores. By the time of the Normandy invasion they were somewhat eclipsed by larger craft but eighty-three operated on the British beaches, and two more supported the Americans. *LCS(M) 101* was damaged in launching but carried on, taking the forward observation officer into position off Nan White Beach in the Juno sector by 0730 on D-Day. She stayed in position for three quarters of an hour, and then landed the forward observation officer as no other craft was available. They took off some men whose LCA had been sunk, then hit a mine and two men were wounded, but all were rescued.

The support craft continued to take part in operations which did not involve LCAs. In April 1945, the 902nd LCS(M) Flotilla patrolled among the islands of the North Scheldt estuary to prevent German midget submarines and motor boats attacking shipping on the way to Antwerp. The LCA was not used much in the Far East, but two LCS(M)s supported commando assault in the Arakan in Burma in December 1944, using guns and smoke. At the very end of the war against Japan, two from the venerable *Glenearn* led a force of thirty amphibious Landing Vehicle, Tracked (LVT) up river to Port Swettenham.

The standard crew of an LCS(M) 3 was one officer and ten men. In *Glengyle* in 1942, one of the two SLCs had a sub-lieutenant RNVR on board as boat officer, and the other had a warrant boatswain. Each had a leading seaman as coxswain, a stoker and eight other seamen, mostly gunners. Royal Marines were used as gunners with seamen to handle the craft, and later the marines came to man the whole craft.

HEDGEROW

The LCAs could be fitted with a weapon known as Hedgerow, which was a reduced version of the Hedgehog mortars used by anti-submarine vessels. It was described to a conference in June 1943.

> This is a spigot mo[r]tar weapon fitted in an L.C.A. with the object of providing a means of dealing with blast-actuated anti-tank mines and wire during the first flight of the assault before infantry are ashore and within the immediate area above high water mark. The equipment will clear a lane in a minefield of the present type of German Teller Mines 120 yards in depth and 30 feet wide, with one salvo. Within its limitations (seaward end of the lane 100 yards for the firing point) it appears that this equipment is the only one at present available which will clear paths through beach anti-tank mines and works during the first phase of the assault, when the assault forces are likely to be under heavy fire.
>
> It also appears to be a useful form of "softening" weapon in its potential use against strong points within its limited range.[3]

The limitations proved too severe for some officers, who demanded a requirement 'To clear a lane through a minefield of Tellermines (42) 90% effective, the lane to be 15 to 20 feet wide and 80 yards long, the furthest to fall 380 yards from the bow of the craft.' Others wanted to be able to vary the range so that the craft did not have to fire from a fixed position, but that was regarded as a long-term project. Trials were held at Studland Bay in Dorset in December. Four LCAs fired against live minefields, with mixed results. The weapon was reasonably successful against barbed wire and had a limited use against Mark IV mines, although no clear lane through them was established; against Mark V mines, only one in thirty was destroyed. Admittedly these were superior to most of the mines used by the Germans, but it did not augur well.

Nevertheless, development proceeded. Hedgerows had already been used at Salerno in September, when *LCA 403* fired a salvo at Red Beach in co-operation with a landing craft rocket. She then offered to fire against Green Beach but that was declined and she fired into the port of Salerno. 'Neither salvo', it was reported, 'was very effective'. It was a similar story with *LCA 802*, which fired onto Sugar Amber Beach at a range of eighty yards to little effect, and was accidentally rammed on the way out. Three of the craft were towed to the landings at Anzio in January 1944, but one had already been put out of action by its own structural weakness after only three bombs were fired during training, and the others were too slow in slipping their tows and did not get into action in time.

An LCA(HR) had a crew of four – coxswain, firing number, motor mechanic and spare hand. It carried twenty-four spare rounds for reloading. Sub-Lieutenant Harper describes the test firing of a salvo.

> They were fired by a ripple switch; the operator turned a handle and the bombs went away in pairs in rapid succession. At first we had to stand on deck and watch the shower exploding on the beach, but after one of our young signalmen had been killed by a piece of shrapnel we took care to keep low when firing.[4]

Despite the problems, there were great hopes in the Hedgerow for the invasion of Normandy, where beach mines and obstacles were far more numerous than in any other landing. Forty-five set off for each of the British beaches, towed by LCTs. All encountered trouble on the way across due to bad weather. Of the nine craft of 592 Flotilla under Captain de Spon RM, five foundered, two broke adrift and were missing, another was found at sea and towed back to base, and only *LCA(HR) 976* under Lieutenant F H Penfold got to the beaches as planned. Once there, she slipped the tow and followed in the LCT. She fired her salvo and hit the beach almost immediately afterwards. Penfold believed that the pattern extended right up the beach and set fire to one of the houses behind, clearing a track that the infantry were able to follow, although this was not confirmed by any other evidence. In general, only about a dozen craft made it to the beaches, but Nan White in the Juno sector was quite well provided. Four Hedgerows fired their mortars there, plus five more on Nan Red. They were attacked with machine gun and mortar fire and replied with 2in mortars. One flotilla officer was full of praise for them. 'They dashed in at exactly the right moment and planted their bombs well up the beach. One succeeded in placing his stick right across the Bernieres strongpoint.' Another reported:

> Just as we were about to touch down two L.C.A, (HR)s came up on my starboard side and with great deliberation planted their bombs among the beach defences. This was of great assistance and must have had a terrifically demoralising effect on the enemy gun crews. Immediately the L.C.A. (HR)s withdrew the enemy opened fire from all points, some machine guns using tracer and some not. It occurred to me at this stage that the enemy knew there were nothing but Oerlikons to fear from L.C.Ts; that he deliberately waited until the L.C.A. (HR)s withdrew before he opened fire.[5]

However, these were comparatively small results over the many beaches, and the LCA(HR)s suffered much damage from rough seas and their own weapons. Some had their bottoms almost blown out by firing their weapons, and all the survivors showed signs of wear. The captain of *Empire Lance* reported: 'The L.C.A. (H.R'S) were all in bad shape when they returned for hoisting being considerably waterlogged, and one craft was hoisted just as it was about to founder. The crews, however, were all safe and in one piece, though a little damp and tired.' Overall, the LCT(HR) cannot be considered a success. Its force was puny compared with the rockets fired by landing craft rocket over the same beaches, and the LCA hull was simply not seaworthy enough for a voyage across the English Channel in rough weather, or to bear the weight of mortar firing on this scale.

OBSTACLE CLEARANCE UNITS

Another LCA task for the Normandy invasion was to work with Landing Craft Obstruction Clearance Units (LCOCUs or Loc-Us). Twelve units were trained, half of these Navy, half Royal Marines. Each had an officer, petty officer or NCO and eleven men, all trained underwater swimmers known as frogmen, who used a modified version of the Davis submarine escape apparatus. At the Combined Operations Experimental Establishment (COXE) at Appledore in North Devon, they trained in placing explosive charges to destroy obstacles – the most difficult, Element C, needed thirty-six charges to destroy a ten feet by ten feet by fourteen feet structure.

But, in practice, there were delays to the landings and the tide was higher than expected, while the weather was far worse. On Sword Beach it was reported:

Obstacles on the beach at La Riviere in Normandy.

Casualties to personnel (which were at their peak between 0800 and 0900), and the rapid rise of the tide, beat the obstacle clearers in their task. The L.C.O.C.U. teams found only one channel on each beach ready to be buoyed out to seaward. When this had been accomplished, attempts were made to

carry on with work on submerged obstacles; but the surf was too heavy to control the L.C.A. from which they worked and there was constant danger to the divers in the continual arrival of more and more flights bearing down upon them and driving in wherever a space clear of other beached craft could be found.[6]

As the tide rose on the morning of D-Day the LCOCUs gave up their primary task and went ashore to help the Royal Engineers units clearing obstacles there, and to resume work as the tide fell. All of this meant that obstacle clearance was slow, even where the units arrived on time.

LCA(OC) 1210 claimed to be the first craft to touch down on King Beach in the Gold sector. Lieutenant Hargreaves, in command of the unit, stood in front of the craft exposed to enemy fire and directed it in through the obstacles. They spent the next five days working on clearance, during which the coxswain, Sergeant A G Buckland, had to manoeuvre his craft through the obstacles many times in bad weather, and the crew had to fend for themselves as they had no living facilities on board. Leading Seaman A C Austin was killed by machine gun or mortar fire on the morning of D-Day, while AB Hirst was severely wounded when he was trying to clear the propeller of an LCT and someone started the engines.[7]

The LCAs had done their best in difficult circumstances, but there was a feeling that they were not large enough for the task and they should be fitted out to carry more stores. It was also pointed out that the LCOCUs did not come together with their LCA crews until very late in the day, and it would be better if they had trained together, because they had to work very closely as a team.

BEACH PARTIES

Another task was to land the beach parties that controlled the flow of ships, men, vehicles and stores in every landing from Madagascar onwards. Only the advance party would land in LCAs, the rest would come later in larger craft with their equipment, but it was difficult in the early stages of a landing, for example in Normandy. On Nan White Beach in the Juno sector, a landing by one LCA was 'effected exactly at the pre-arranged position …'. The other LCA had difficulty getting in. It lost sight of the first LCA, its crew 'put too much faith in the assurances of the officer in charge, who had already beached once, and was taken some half-a-mile to the Eastward of the pre-arranged position, where the LCA struck a mine on a Hedgehog about 30 yards from the water's edge and sank forthwith'. The party waded ashore with most of their gear and walked to the beachmaster's headquarters.

On one beach in the Sword sector, the advance parties had even greater difficulties as they landed with the assault infantry. Three out of the eight men were killed or wounded. There was great congestion as obstacles remained uncleared and beach exits were not yet open. When an LCT arrived with the heavy equipment, it was very difficult to unload because of the depth of water. The official report complained:

It is hardly surprising therefore to find the old, old cry repeated in all reports covering this period: 'The Naval Beach parties were conspicuous by their absence …', 'No craft was flagged in until late in the day …', 'No beach signs could be seen …'.[8]

LANDING IN SURF

By October 1942, the Pacific War against Japan had been going for less than one year, but already the Americans were on the offensive on Guadalcanal, and even the hard-pressed British were thinking about a return. They knew that the LCA, designed for different conditions in northwest Europe and the Mediterranean, would not behave well in Pacific surf and began to look at ways of improving it. One boat was fitted with a false stern and tested at Durban and later at Bombay. It had some success in landing, but it was difficult to retract in surf, and dangerous to turn it round as it might be hit broadside on by a wave and broach to. The British authorities considered American methods.

Powerful engines and a good hull design have rendered possible an improved technique which has been evolved by the Americans during this war. The craft approaches the beach at high speed and so retains manoeuvrability and steerage way until beached. An anchor is not used and she remains stern onto the sea and surf by going ahead on the engines when beached and using her rudder. To retract she goes full speed astern every time she is waterborne or nearly waterborne by a wave. Immediately the craft is fully waterborne she goes full speed ahead with the helm hard over and so turns quickly in the surf. She then proceeds at moderate speed right through the surf and head on to it.[9]

An LCA modified to operate in surf, with the steering position aft.

The standard American craft, the LCV(P), had a single engine generating 225 or 250 brake horsepower, while the LCA had two with a total of 130bhp. Nevertheless by the end of 1943, when it was possible to see an end to the war in Europe, more attempts were made to redesign the LCA for service in the Pacific. It was difficult to find a British site where the boats could be tested – surf six feet high with a ten second period was expected there but the best British areas, in North Devon and Cornwall, offered an average of three feet and a maximum of five feet. Nevertheless, K C Barnaby, the original designer of the LCA, was contacted at Thornycroft and a few improvements were suggested. The wheelhouse was moved aft to a position between the two engines to give the helmsman a better view astern and more protection from spray. It also allowed him to operate the engines directly without going through the stoker, so that he could respond faster to the waves as they came in. New propellers and larger rudders were fitted. A breakwater was added right aft and a much larger and higher winch was fitted for the kedge anchor, but nothing was done about the relatively low engine power, and the basic hull shape remained unchanged except for some rounding in the stern. *LCA 123* was modified to this pattern and tested at Padstow in spring 1945. They were unsuccessful in several respects.

> The engine power of the craft is still quite inadequate to give the sudden kick off the beach when the craft is momentarily waterborne or to provide that acceleration necessary to enable her to get away from the beach before being broached by successive waves. Furthermore owing to the small water pumps and diminutive nature of the water cooling system, sand is still very liable to get into this system
>
> The fitting of a hand operated kedge winch and the substitution of a wire cable for the grass line used hitherto have proved disappointing. In trials it was found that the operation of winding in the kedge line was hazardous on account of the spray and sea breaking over the stern. The time taken to recover the anchor by this means delayed the turning round of the craft.
>
> The turning circle of the craft, though improved by the enlarged rudder area, is still a long way short of the L.C.P.(L) or L.C.V.(P), and when using engines to assist the turn it is essential that the R.P.M. on each engine is the same, otherwise the craft will surge either ahead or astern.[10]

The engine power was not enough for retraction, and the open well-deck in the bow between the armoured doors and the ramp would quickly flood. The changes offered a slight improvement, but it was still far inferior to the LCV(P) in this kind of operation. In May 1945, just after the war in Europe ended, it was concluded, 'Even with the bow decked in the shortcomings of the craft are still such that it must be accepted that the L.C.A cannot be altered sufficiently for her to be considered in any way a surf boat.' It was decided to abandon the attempt and use the American LCV(P), but the war against Japan ended before it became necessary.[11]

OPERATIONS

NARVIK – APRIL 1940

Assault landing craft first saw action after the German invasion of Norway in spring 1940. Four were sent out to join the flagging campaign to recapture the key northern port of Narvik. Captain 'Blondie' Hasler of the Royal Marines (later famous for the 'Cockleshell Heroes' raid on Bordeaux and as an ocean yachtsman) found their crews bivouacking 'in a state of some savagery, having no officer to look after them' but he had to admire the ratings' ingenuity in camouflaging their vessels with foliage. It had already been decided to withdraw allied forces that were suffering heavily due to lack of air cover, but a diversion was needed. An attack was planned near the village of Bjerkvik at the head of a fjord north of Narvik. The British army was reluctant to attack, so two battalions of the French Foreign Legion were deployed, although their officers admitted that '… it is all very difficult, we are used to travelling on camels across the desert and here you give us boats to travel across the water'. A scratch force was put together including some local craft or *Skoyters*, known as 'puffers' to the British, the four ALCs, three of the unsatisfactory MLC 10s of 1926 and one more modern MLC 1. It assembled in Ofotfjord, where British warships had scored their only major success of the campaign in mid-April. The MLC 1 and the ALCs would make the twenty miles to the landing site under their own power, the old MLC 10s would be carried in the battleship *Resolution*. The first flight was restricted to 290 men because of shortage of craft to land them – this was considered risky because it would take three-quarters of an hour to land a second wave. It was planned to land tanks first, but it took a long time to hoist out the MLC 10, and the LCAs landed their ninety troops on a beach east of the village, watched from a distance by Maund who had helped conceive them.

> We could see the dark forms, like so many ants, after five hours in the L.C.A., run out of their craft, open out and, without a moment's pause, advance across and over the knoll that covered the village from the west.

Fortunately, resistance was slight. Narvik was captured, but soon given up as part of a general withdrawal. It was agreed that a larger supply of suitable landing craft might have made a difference to the campaign.

The landing of such a small advanced party on a hostile shore entailed considerable risk; and in view of the likelihood of such operations having to be repeated in other theatres of war, it is urgently necessary that an ample supply of modern landing craft should be provided without further delays. It is unfair to expect any troops to undertake such hazardous operations with such inadequate means.[1]

DUNKIRK – MAY 1940

By this time, the allied armies were retreating in France, and the evacuation from Dunkirk had begun. The ALCs, with shallow draught and bow doors, were far more suitable for this than the 'little ships' that became the heroes of British mythology, but they were few in number. At 2100 on 26 May, the ISTDC received orders to send all available landing craft and eight ALCs were loaded into the merchant ship *Clan Macalister* at Southampton. Led by Commander R A Cassidi, they arrived at Dunkirk at about 1000 on 29 May, but, while unloading, two were damaged as the parent ship was rocked by the wash of a passing destroyer, and these were put out of action. Another ALC and four MLCs arrived later. For the remaining six landed from *Clan Macalister*, Cassidi soon gave orders that the two junior officers and the coxswains should use their initiative in choosing beaches and he saw nothing of them for days afterwards except for a brief meeting with *ALC 17*. *ALC 5* under Cassidi himself was overrun by French troops and some had to be forced off before the craft could float. She then transferred to La Panne beach and began to ferry British troops out to ships lying offshore. She made three trips per hour carrying fifty men, except when interrupted by air raids, and took off a total of 750 men. She shifted back to Dunkirk and made many more runs in the dark. Commander Cassidi estimated that she carried between two and three thousand troops in all.

ALC 16 was commanded by RNVR Sub-Lieutenant Wilcoxson:

A.L.C. 16 was the first boat to be hoisted out, and proceeded straight inshore to the beach near Old Dunkirk where she evacuated British troops. After making some seven trips successfully, she was boarded by a mob of French soldiers, who overwhelmed the boat to such an extent that she became partially swamped, the starboard battery was flooded and both engines failed.

Eventually sufficient French troops were evicted to enable A.L.C. 16 to be floated off, and the port engine started. Unfortunately in going astern off the beach she rode over the anchor, and did such damage to the port shafting that the port stern tube was loosened in the framework of the hull, and water poured into the boat.

Continually pumping and bailing, A.L.C. 16 continued running for a further hour and a half evacuating troops. However, damage to the boat was such that Sub. Lieut. Wilcoxson thought it advisable for the boat to be towed back to England for repairs.

With this in view he went alongside and put troops aboard H.M.S. Bideford, Sub. Lieut. Wilcoxson at the same time going inboard to arrange a tow.

While lying alongside Bideford a heavy attack was made by enemy dive bombers, and Bideford struck aft. A terrific explosion resulted within a few feet of A.L.C. 16.

The wooden portions of the boat forward and aft were blown to fragments, the bottom of the boat split lengthways, one of the crew falling through the bottom, but the armoured portion of the boat remained intact, the armour closing in overhead. Fortunately the boat's crew were crouching down in the armoured part of the craft when the explosion occurred and were completely unscathed. They attribute their survival entirely to the armour protection. ... A.L.C. 16 sank after a few minutes. Unfortunately Sub. Lieut. Wilcoxson, who was aboard H.M.S. *Bideford*, was mortally wounded.[2]

ALC 17, under a coxswain whose name is not recorded, had a similar experience with the French army and was stranded for three hours as the tide fell. The coxswain then called on the assistance of British troops with fixed bayonets to stop her being overrun again – not the last time an ALC coxswain had to assert himself against superior ranks and numbers. She ferried troops out for the rest of the day and much of the night until her engines gave out and she was towed across the English Channel for repairs. *ALC*s 5, 8 and *16* returned under their own power carrying between ten and twenty-five troops each, because it was not wise to take a full load of thirty-five for such a long and hazardous trip. The others, *ALC*s 8 and 15, were lost on the beaches. Of the ALCs generally, it was pointed out that:

> ... these craft were subjected to very abnormal use; they were invariably overloaded; a great strain was thrown on the engines and clutches owing to the fact that the sea off the beaches at Dunkirk was full of every form of floating obstacle including clothing, equipment, etc., etc., which continually fouled the propellers.[3]

Dakar – September 1940

In August 1940, a force was hastily put together to take the Vichy-held colonial port of Dakar, and the landing ships were the P&O troopship *Ettrick*, the Polish *Sobieski* and the British India Steam Navigation Company's *Kenya* and *Karanja*. Between them they carried fifteen ALCs, two LCMs and one LCS, with three LCAs per ship, except *Sobieski*, which had six. The other davits carried ships' lifeboats which were of little use for landing. Ships went to Scapa Flow for a few days to train their marines in landing techniques, as one of their officers describes:

> Crouched down with blackened faces we would approach a beach at speed, the rear-mounted engines suddenly going full astern as we passed through the line of breakers. The rattle of the ramp going down was the signal for me to run forward at the head of my men who fanned out on each side as they raced through the darkness for the foreshore.[4]

The force arrived off Dakar on 23 September. A small Free French force went ashore in ships' boats and was rebuffed but the main landing was cancelled, partly because there were not enough landing craft to deal with any resistance.

Early commando raids

In March 1941, commandos carried out a much more successful raid on the Lofoten Islands on the approaches to Narvik, and planned to destroy a fish oil factory with a certain amount of strategic value. The landing ships (still known as raiding craft carriers in official accounts) were *Prins Albert* and *Prinses Josephine Charlotte*, each carrying three ALCs transferred from *Keren*, one SLC and four R-boats that had originally been *Prins Albert*'s flotilla. The ALCs were to go in first, supported by the gunfire of corvettes which were more used to anti-submarine work in the Atlantic. The R-boats were in reserve. The raid went according to plan for once and was a complete success. The fish oil factory was destroyed, more than 200 prisoners were taken and 300 Norwegian volunteers were taken back. Morale was restored and the raid was highly publicised.

But raids did not always go so well. On 19 and 20 April 1941, *Glengyle*'s and *Glenearn*'s ALCs supported the army in North Africa by landing commandos fifty miles behind the enemy lines at Bardia in Libya. It claimed a place in history as the first raid from specialised ships, but Evelyn Waugh was less kind as the raid proved largely pointless due to faulty intelligence.

> The town was deserted, the only vehicles were abandoned trucks, the guns had been destroyed some weeks before when we evacuated the town. No other use was made of the road, which had been reported as frequented, during our three hours occupation.[5]

Many things went wrong. One party of sixty men got lost and had to be left behind. One ALC was stranded and abandoned, another was lost without a compass and was left behind to find her own way back – over seventy miles.

The evacuation from Greece – April 1941

The engineers and shipwrights on board the *Glen*s barely had time to repair their damaged LCAs, when they were needed for another large-scale evacuation, and this time the landing craft would play a central role. Greece had fallen under the German onslaught and British forces had to be withdrawn. On the night of 24–25 April, each of *Glengyle*'s landing craft made several trips off Raphti carrying an average of forty-five men, while the MLCs carried 140 men on each of eleven trips. *Glenearn* operated off Nauplia.

> At 1855/24 proceeded towards Nauplia arriving off Tenagia Point and anchoring at 2155 on 24th.
>
> All landing craft were at once sent to the harbour and embarkation commenced. The smooth functioning of this operation was marred only by two incidents.
>
> No 9 A.L.C. managed to get athwart the bows of HYACINTH which was passing up the Port side too close to the ship, and was rammed and capsized. It is feared some troops were drowned.
>
> The inefficient work of the tank landing craft ...

> By 0230/25 the congestion on board was so great that I was compelled to stop embarking troops. Number on board approximately 5,100, including 2 German prisoners and 30 cot cases of wounded.[6]

They were taken to Suda Bay in Crete. Meanwhile six ALCs from *Glenroy*, repairing from bomb damage in Alexandria, were sent to evacuate troops from Megara and they loaded them into cruisers and destroyers there.

Glenearn was damaged by bombing but launched ten ALCs in the evening of 26 April, and they motored twenty six miles north to Monemvasia while the parent ship was towed away. They arrived at 0430 next day, but the troops they were to meet were not yet there, and it was impossible to operate in daylight due to enemy air superiority. They were placed half-a-mile apart along the beaches and hidden in undergrowth. An A-lighter, or tank landing craft, had been bombed, so the ALCs were the only means of evacuation when members of the New Zealand 6th Brigade arrived on the 28th. After dark, they took the wounded out to four waiting destroyers, only to find that there was no means of lifting them on board and they had to be brought back. The rest of the men were embarked from stone jetties because there was no suitable beach, and ferried out sixty at a time as the operation got under way, and eventually the wounded were put on the cruiser HMS *Ajax*. The evacuation of 4000 men was complete by around 0300 next day and the ALCs were left behind, only partly destroyed because the captain of *Ajax* wanted to get away.

Glengyle landed 5750 men on Crete and was back off Greece by the night of the 26th to 27th, when her ALCs operated off C Beach at Raphina in a force 4 wind with slight swell on the beach, and moderate off shore.

> Embarkation commenced at 2215 hours and ceased at 0200 hours. Slow, due to swell and the distance of the Glenship off shore (1½ miles). Although the number of troops planned to be lifted on this night was 3000 over 4000 men arrived on the beach. The Brigadier in command, expecting that all men would be embarked, destroyed all his guns on arrival at the beach in accordance with his orders. By 0200, however, the weather had deteriorated to such an extent that no further embarkation that night was possible, if Glengyle was to make her rendezvous with A.A. escort. An unsatisfactory feature was that the Beachmaster and beach party themselves embarked in spite of their being 900 men on shore.[7]

On D Beach at Raphti, Boatswain Aveling took charge of *Glengyle's* beach party, which was landed without any blankets, weapons or equipment. Because they were ashore longer than expected, they had to take supplies from troops as they were embarked. There were not enough signallers or seamen, and beachmasters had to row themselves around the beach. Fortunately the weather was good.

> Twice the budgeted number of troops arrived. Delays due to (i) strandings of craft due to cox'ns allowing them to beach empty but mainly to inefficiency of beach party. Tired troops had to be disembarked in order to refloat lighters.

LCAs return to their parent ships after the Lofoten Islands raid.

(ii) At other times, soldiers did not appear quickly enough to fill craft owing to underestimation of capacity of craft for rapid turnarounds. Beach was however cleared.[8]

Three thousand, three hundred men out of 4100 were successfully embarked that night. Fifty thousand men were evacuated from Greece – around 80 per cent of those landed – and the ALCs handled nearly half of them.

CRETE – MAY 1941

The British determination to hold on to Crete did not last long after the island was invaded by German paratroopers and airborne infantry. On 27 May, just a month after the loss of Greece, it was decided to evacuate yet again. *Glengyle* had landed one of the last parties of reinforcements with great difficulty on the 22nd, and now there were doubts about sending an unarmoured ship back to take men off, putting 3000 troops at mortal risk. These were overridden and she joined the evacuation at Sphakia in the south of the island on the night of the 29–30 May, with seven warships on the second night of the evacuation. *Glengyle*'s LCAs operated from the small beach, and these were assisted by two more that had been brought by the cruiser *Perth*. Other craft, such as ship's boats, were not used because of restrictions on space. Troops were even more traumatised than at Dunkirk, by the constant bombing and machine gunning from the air and the passage in the LCA was a huge relief.

> Exactly 2 am, a light flashed out at sea and a few minutes later a landing craft loomed through the darkness. A short journey, and we were scrambling up boarding nets on to the SS *Glengyle*. 'Cocoa and cigarettes in the officers' mess just down the passage' said a calm voice. After an interlude I fell asleep in a passageway, my tin hat (my only possession) my pillow.[9]

Over 6000 men were taken off – the largest on any of the five nights of evacuation – and more than one third of the 16,500 men evacuated. If any of the soldiers had once laughed at the LCA crews' lack of training at Inveraray, they had cause to be grateful now. The transports were grossly overcrowded as they headed back to Egypt.

> You can imagine how we were packed out, there was no sleep for any of the crew, and we went several days without any. With these numbers on board, the state of the ship can well be imagined. All craft on the davits were manned by those troops fit enough to do so, assisted with small arms to beat off air attacks. Many casualties were received amongst these men but we did not receive any damage, and soon became known throughout the East Mediterranean as a 'lucky ship'. On this trip especially the medical and supply branches of the ship worked night and day to look after this huge number of men.[10]

More commando raids

In September 1941, the LSI (Small) *Prince Leopold* used four of her eight ALCs to land commandos on two sites on the Normandy coast that would become very familiar three years later. She waited several hours for their return but missed them partly due to a navigational error. The ALCs eventually made their separate ways back to England. It was realised that it was unwise to leave a landing ship for so long off an enemy coast, and for the next raid, on Dives in Normandy, *Prince Leopold* lowered her ALCs and then withdrew. The troops were landed on what was thought to be a suitable spot, which turned out to be wide and sticky, and the troops had to return to the ALCs before they could reach solid ground.

Commandos returned to Norwegian waters at Christmas 1941, when *Prince Charles* and *Prince Leopold* used their assault craft for a raid on the island of Vaagsø. Both ships had launched their ALCs by 0842 on 27 December and one of four groups was approaching its objective on Maaløy Island five and a half minutes later. One landing craft was hit by a smoke bomb dropped by an aircraft but there were few casualties as the troops were put ashore. The landing craft were used to ferry casualties, prisoners and Norwegian volunteers out to the ships and began withdrawal, which was completed by 1434. The operation claimed a success in killing around 150 Germans, taking 102 prisoners plus four Norwegian collaborators, and bringing back seventy-seven Norwegian volunteers. It destroyed various guns and installations, and put a fish oil factory out of action. It also helped create a fear in the German high command that the Allies were planning a full-scale

Paratroopers train in withdrawal by LCA in preparation for the Bruneval raid.

invasion of Norway, which caused much diversion of manpower. But German reprisals were so savage that they deterred the Free Norwegians from supporting any more raids such as this.

The Bruneval raid in February 1942 was unusual for LCAs, in that they were to pick up parachute troops who had landed on the French coast to attack a radar station. *Prins Albert* was ordered to anchor twenty miles offshore and launch her six LCAs and two LCSs, which were then towed to a position three miles offshore to move in and await contact with the army. Despite the lack of a proper dress rehearsal and the doubts of the army, contact was made by Verey light from a mile and a half out. The Germans then opened a heavy fire that was answered by the LCSs and the LCAs, each of which carried eight Bren guns, creating an 'indescribable' amount of noise. The troops had to wade thigh-deep through five or ten yards of water as the officers herded their men into the boats as quickly as they could, for they could not stay long with the state of the tide. They brought three prisoners and parts of

Troops disembarking from LCA 164 *in Tamatave, Madagascar.*

the enemy radar set, essential for intelligence purposes. One of the LCAs was grossly overcrowded with sixty-eight soldiers as well as the captured parts and it had to be shoved off by the soldiers. Its engine then broke down, and it was towed while the stoker repaired it in very difficult conditions. All got off safely and rendezvoused with the motor gunboats and with *Prins Albert*, which brought them home. Two signallers, who had been landed in the wrong place but were in contact by radio, were left behind and it was deemed too dangerous to go back for them.

MADAGASCAR – MAY 1942

From early 1942, the assault landing craft (ALC) was renamed to become landing craft assault (LCA), to conform to American practice. It was a symbolic moment, for until then the ALC had shone during retreats, the LCA would become increasingly prominent in attacks. Early in 1942, it was decided to invade the Vichy-French colony of Madagascar to prevent the Japanese acquiring a fine harbour in the Indian Ocean. A force set off in what was to prove Britain's longest range invasion of the war, with the LSIs *Winchester Castle*, *Keren* and *Karanja* carrying LCAs, *Sobieski* with R-boats and the converted tanker *Derwentdale* carrying LCMs to launch tanks. The force was landed in the bay behind the main port of Diego Suarez on the morning of 5 May against moderate opposition. The port was secured within two days, but it was still necessary to conquer the rest of the island. *Empire Pride*, *Dunera* and *Dilmara* carried twenty LCAs to attack the main port, Tamatave, while other ships had six LCMs and eight LCPs. The first flight hit Red Beach early in the morning of 10 September, within yards of its target. There was some delay with hoisting out LCMs, but all the LCAs had landed their troops and returned to the parent ships within about an hour. A few hours later, more LCAs assaulted Green Beach to the south. Unusually, *Empire Pride*'s eight LCAs touched down against the sea wall rather than a beach. Leading Seaman Legrow, one of the coxswains, was recommended by his flotilla officer for an award.

> In accordance with the pre-arranged plan, the 8 L.C.A. of EMPIRE PRIDE Flotilla had formed line abreast when approx. [?] mile off the beach. My own boat was on the left and Ldg. Sea. Legrow was on the extreme right.
>
> When approximately 250 yards from the Beach, hostile machine gun fire commenced. All boats brought up bows on to the sea wall. The army officer in Legrow's boat, together with 2 Bren gunners, scrambled up on to the wall, the two latter commencing to fire at a house slightly to the right on the front.
>
> The remaining troops appear to have experienced some difficulty in getting on to the sea wall and Legrow, seeing this, put his engines to slow ahead, his wheel amidships and set up his scaling ladder against the wall. He then climbed on to the top of the wall and steadied the ladder whilst pulling the troops up.
>
> In view of the fact that firing was coming from the house to the right of the line of boats and would naturally be concentrated on the nearest boat, and that Legrow was

'Dieppe - withdrawal from Beach'

LCAs withdrawing
troops from Dieppe.

An LCA, fitted with smoke
canisters, rescues a downed
airman after the Dieppe raid.

completely exposed and only a matter of 50 or 100 yards away, I have considered his behaviour worthy of a mention.[11]

On 23 April, a further landing was necessary, during which six LCAs were grounded and could not be refloated, but the beaches were secured without opposition. The Vichy forces on the island finally surrendered on 5 November.

DIEPPE – AUGUST 1942

But it was not all success, for in August 1942 a large-scale raid was launched on the French port of Dieppe. It was misconceived and ill-planned on many levels. Air superiority had now been achieved and so it was very different from Narvik, Dunkirk, Greece and Crete, but the enemy defences in front of a major port were not neutralised. Nine of the LSIs, including *Glengyle* and most of the Dutch and Belgian ships, were used to transport sixty LCAs to five beaches, one in the town itself and two more on either side. A force of seventy-four landing craft personnel (large) (LCP(L)) or R-boats crossed the channel under their own power, with two dozen tank landing craft and supporting destroyers and warships. The landing took place at dawn but the enemy was ready and the Royal Marines and Canadian troops were slaughtered.

> As we touched down, we heard a sound you could never forget: a tremendous 'rat-tat-tat' as blistering volleys of machine-gun bullets raked the armoured door of my LCA. That gun was trained directly on us. The naval commander wanted to know why I was not getting out – he said he had to get back to England! With that, the fire switched and out we went. There was no hesitation by the troops who followed me. However, only ten of us made it to the wall. [12]

There were plenty of recriminations and some of the troops claimed that the landing craft crews had not behaved well in dangerous conditions. According to a Canadian lance-corporal:

> The LCA did not beach but was within twenty-five yards of the beach. The men had to swim in about seven feet of water to reach shore. We rushed out of the craft with our mortar, which was on the dolly and weighed about four hundred pounds. When we hit the water, the dolly sank instantly. We struggled to move it. Many of the detachment disappeared and I found myself alone trying to pull it onto the beach.

It was decided to withdraw and the naval force commander ordered that the un-armoured LCTs and LCPs should not be used in the intense fire – the LCAs and LCMs from the landing ships were sent into an inferno to get out as many men as possible. On the western inner flank at Pourville, *LCAs 250* and *315* made three trips and took men from the South Saskatchewan Regiment out to LCTs and destroyers until after noon. On the main beaches off Dieppe, *LCA 186* picked up about thirty men swimming in the water and was the last to leave. A thousand men were taken off, but overall the Canadians suffered 68 per cent casualties and prisoners, and the Royal Marines and American Rangers also suffered. So too did the LCAs – seventeen, or 28 per cent, were lost.

NORTH AFRICA

As the Vichy forces finally surrendered on Madagascar on 5 November, several huge convoys were approaching the coast of North Africa, for the Americans were about to land near Casablanca and at Safi, and the British inside the Mediterranean at Algiers and Oran. It was the largest operation mounted so far and the training camps had been emptied as partly trained crews were embarked in LSIs. The Combined Operations organisation was under considerable strain as the demands increased. Fifteen LSIs had originally been requested for the operation, twenty-five eventually sailed. The planners had asked for ninety-one LCAs with their crews, but now they needed 140.

The lack of training showed and several of the LCA flotillas got into

Unloading ammunition at Arzeu during the North Africa landings.

difficulties. Off Algiers there was a westerly current that caused many landing ships and craft to arrive in the wrong place. Fortunately there was little resistance from the Vichy French. The three landings in the Oran area had similar difficulties. West of the town, *Queen Emma*'s and *Princess Beatrix*'s ten LCAs formed only a small part of the total of thirty-nine craft, which were mostly LCP and LCMs. *Queen Emma*'s five craft failed to find Green Beach. Lieutenant Thomson, already a hero of the Dieppe raid, was commended for his efforts:

As senior flotilla officer of the flotillas belonging to H.M. Ships 'QUEEN EMMA' and 'PRINCESS BEATRIX' he was charged with the handling, deploying and beaching of the first flight at Mersa Bou Zedjar (X Beach Oran) at 0100 on 8th November 1942. The navigation during the run was not to be his responsibility. A Motor Launch with a special pilot on board was to undertake this duty. In the event, the arrangements did not go according to plan. The craft were lowered in the wrong place and the flotillas could not see each other, and the navigational M.L. never appeared. Lieutenant Thomson took prompt measures. He found the other flotilla, formed them in order,

undertook the navigation himself and proceeded inshore at full speed. After making a landfall and detaching the other flotilla, he beached his flotilla and landed his troops at the right place.[13]

The LCPs from *Batory* landed first – they were less suitable for an opposed landing, which might have caused problems had there been any resistance. Closer to Oran, *Glengyle* served as headquarters ship and carried eleven LCAs, an LCS and two LCMs, while *Monarch of Bermuda* carried twelve more LCAs out of a total landing force of forty-five. The troops from *Monarch of Bermuda* were embarked via ladders, the rungs of which turned out to be too far apart. This caused delay so that the LCAs from her and *Glengyle* landed sixteen minutes late, and the LCMs grounded on undiscovered sandbars offshore.

The third landing, east of Oran, was much larger and involved 29,000 troops, 2400 vehicles and eight LSIs plus the LCM carrier *Derwentdale*. It deployed eighty-five landing craft, of which sixty-eight were LCAs and three were LCSs. The first flight of assault craft heading for Z Green beach lost cohesion despite being led in by a motor launch – the first of its craft landed twelve minutes before H-hour, the last landed ten minutes after. In *Ulster Monarch*:

At about 2330 on the 7th November 1942, when in a position 7 miles North East of the port of Arzou on the French Algerian Coast, the pipe, 'Hands to Invasion Stations' was piped over the loud hailer. ... L.C.S. (M) 31 took station abeam and to port of the 50th Flotilla who were disposed in two columns; the five L.C.A.'s from 'Ulster Monarch' to port and the 4 L.C.A.s from 'Royal Ulsterman' to starboard. Within a mile and a half of Cape Carbon the Flotilla formed line abreast, the L.C.S. taking station to starboard of 'Royal Ulsterman's' boats. The forming of line abreast was delayed by the bad station keeping of the rear boats of the columns who were far astern of station. The beaching was uncertain in that the boats lost touch with each other and as a result a few, including the L.C.S., found themselves facing cliffs and rocks.

I ordered the L.C.S. to go to port and being slightly ahead of the others warned them of the danger. I then proceeded closer to Cape Carbon and made the beach. After landing the Doctor a course was steered parallel to the coast with the intention of making for Arzou harbour. However three loaded L.C.A's were sighted apparently searching for the beach. It was then about 0125. The L.C.S. guided these craft (from 'Royal Ulsterman') to the beach, and then proceeded on her course.[14]

Again there was no opposition, which was fortunate. Oran surrendered fifty-nine hours after the invasion began.

SICILY – JULY 1943

The invasion of Sicily in July 1943 was the first direct assault on an enemy's homeland, and the biggest and most complex yet. British and American forces assembled from Scotland, Egypt, Algeria and Malta. The British were to land on beaches to the north and west of Cape Passero in the southeastern corner of the island, the Americans further to the west. Again the LCAs were expected to lead the way on the British beaches, although there was a danger that they might be upstaged by new craft that were coming into service – the amphibious DUKW; the landing craft infantry (large) (LCI(L)), which could carry 200 men; the landing craft tank (LCT), which was available in increasing numbers and could carry up to nine tanks; and the much larger landing ship tank (LST) which could cross an ocean with up to eighteen. In the early days, as in Norway and at Dakar, the lack of LCAs had determined the course of operations. Now they were in mass production and there was no shortage, while LSIs could be improvised quickly from merchant shipping. It was shortages of larger vessels, especially LSTs, which placed constraints on allied strategy.

But none of the new types was intended for the initial assault and the LCA was still expected to lead the way in. This time it was the weather that interfered with the best laid plans, because a sudden and unexpected wind of force 4 to 6 blew up from the northwest in the afternoon of the 9th, leaving a very disturbed sea on the western beaches where the landings were to take place next day. Conditions were felt most strongly in an LCA as soon as it was lowered.

Down, down we went, towards the swirling waves; every now and then our steel landing-craft, weighing come fourteen tons, would thud and crash against the ship's hull. Then, with a splash, we were in the water rising and falling in an alarming manner. For a few moments sailors struggled to free the huge steel blocks which were still attached to us. We lay on our faces in case the swinging blocks should crush our skulls.

I learned a great deal about nautical blasphemy ... A final wrench and with a shudder from the darkness of the ship's side.[15]

There were delays in Roger sector of Bark West as commanders decided it was not safe to launch the LCAs in such conditions and adopted an alternative plan to load the men into LCTs and land them by DUKW when nearer the beaches. The LCT loaded men from one ship, and then reached *Glengyle*, where it was decided to use the LCAs after all, causing disorder and delay. On Acid North near Syracuse, there was bad bunching among craft and it proved difficult to form up the LCA flotillas, but the first was only ten minutes late in landing. On Acid Centre just to the south, two LCA flotillas were led in by the destroyer *Eskimo*, which took them to within a mile and a half of the beach but had been set too far to the southwards. The LCAs then fell into disorder. Some landed on a different beach, and others were rounded up and sent to the correct beach. On Bark South beach near Cape Passero, Alec Guinness was in command of an LSI(L) that failed to get the delaying signal and he led in a group of craft to be the first to land. The American sector was more sheltered against the weather but some LCAs were stranded on a false beach and the DUKWs used their amphibious qualities to rescue the troops and take them ashore. Fortunately, resistance was slight on all of the beaches because the Italians were on the point of giving up the war and the Germans were further inland.

Although the LCAs had encountered many problems, their role was still recognised. Out of a total of ninety-four embarked, three had been lost on operations. A few were damaged but quickly repaired. Their crews seemed well trained on the whole and it was commented:

> It is natural that a higher state of efficiency and morale will be obtained amongst personnel of the L.C.A. and L.C.P. flotillas than in L.C.M. flotillas, which, except in the case of those carried in [landing ships gantry] and [landing ships carrier] are dispersed among a number of other ships and do not receive the supervision and disciplinary training that is necessary.[16]

The LCI(L) had done well but it was generally agreed that it was not a first wave craft, because it grounded in quite deep water, the men had to disembark down steep ramps, and the craft caught fire easily if hit. The DUKWs were a great success, although their limitations had to be recognised, while the LST was very successful in the build-up stage, but it had to beach in nearly five feet of water and was not suitable for a first wave.

To Italy

On 3 September 1943, allied forces followed the retreating enemy across the Strait of Messina to gain the first (almost literal) toehold on the continent of Europe for the first time since the debacle in Greece. Sub-Lieutenant George Slaughter was an officer in an LCA flotilla:

> [We] steamed across covered by a magnificent barrage from out side. We finally hit the beach after going through a smoke screen; the barrage having lifted a few minutes previously. There was fortunately no opposition on the beaches and I only heard one rifle shot fired at us. The Italians had taken to the hills.[17]

But allied forces there were cut off in a narrow peninsula, and a landing further up Italy was necessary to pursue the campaign. This would prove to be far more difficult as German resistance stiffened, even though the Italians signed an armistice and surrendered their fleet. An operation was hastily thrown together to land in Salerno Bay near Naples on 9 September. The Americans landed on four beaches to the south, the British in three sectors, each with two beaches a few miles further north. At the northern end of the area, a force of British commandos and American Rangers landed in LCAs at 0320, after travelling for just over one hour from their LSIs. They were unopposed and quickly secured the beach while the LCAs returned to get stores. On Red Beach in Uncle sector just to the south, the ships came under fire early in the morning but their American-built LCVPs landed the assault wave while *LCA 403* fired its Hedgerow rockets in support. There was confusion on Green Beach next to it, because a landing craft rocket (LCR) fired her salvo in the wrong place and the LCV(P)s followed this to land their troops there. *LCA 403* had moved south and offered to fire another salvo in support of the troops on Green Beach, but this was declined because it might endanger their own men. Instead, she spotted enemy batteries and directed naval gunfire onto these.

In the Sugar sector the LCAs began lowering at 0130 and began to move off half an hour later, while *LCA 802* went in to fire her Hedgerow. Two craft from *Prinses Astrid* were hit and two soldiers killed but the men were landed on Green and Amber beaches, no more than ten minutes late and with little opposition. In the second waves, the LCAs for Sugar Amber landed on Green instead and this caused much congestion and delay. There were similar errors on the Roger beaches, where the first wave consisted of six LCAs from *Sobieski* and six from *Glengyle*. The beachmaster was landed on Green by mistake and he and his party had to make their way on foot past an enemy battery, from which they could hear voices but were not detected. The second wave of twenty-five LCAs was under way by 0220 and came under fire from a machine gun which was silenced by an LCS. They were fired on again as they left the beach, and *Royal Scotsman*'s flotilla was dive bombed but not hit. Overall, the landings were covered by strong carrier-borne air power and were successful, though the army pressed on too quickly and suffered defeats before taking Naples on 1 October.

ANZIO – JANUARY 1944

Again the front became static and the Allies planned landings on either side of the small port of Anzio south of Rome. British forces were to land to the north on Peter Beach, the Americans to the south on X-ray. For the first time, new types of LST were available, and these could carry six LCAs in davits. It was

LCAs are checked on a dockside before the landings at Anzio.

suggested that these might eventually supplant the LSI in short-range operations, although they had no troop accommodation for long-range operations. But not enough were ready, and some of the LSTs landed amphibious DUKWs instead. This was not successful and highlighted the limitations of craft that were otherwise highly successful – the DUKW was too slow at five knots maximum in the water, and it could not handle steep beaches.

As a result, most of the assault landing work still devolved on the British LSIs. Three, including the ubiquitous *Glengyle*, *Winchester Castle* and the Polish *Sobieski*, were used in the British sector. Five more were used to land American troops by way of their LCAs. Conditions were as good as could be expected. There was a wind of only half a knot and a flat calm, so that *Royal Ulsterman* could disembark her troops through

American troops board an LCA before the Normandy landings.

ASSAULT LANDING CRAFT

her side doors. Tactical surprise was achieved and there was little resistance. Navigation was carefully planned, and one senior officer even complained that too many boats were placed along the route and only got in the way. Just before midnight on 21 January 1944, six LCAs from *Royal Ulsterman* formed up with those from *Princess Beatrix* and were led in to Yellow Beach in the X-Ray sector by an American patrol vessel. They touched down at two in the morning:

> … the only opposition experienced was an occasional shell or heavy mortar-bomb, four of which straddled the craft as they came off the beach after the second flight. No damage being sustained except by a small piece of shrapnel which hit the fifth craft of the line.

In the Peter sector, *LCA 405*, from *Glengyle*, suffered slightly more on the third day when a near miss holed her and set the engines on fire. The fire was put out, all the gear was taken on board other craft and the craft was sent back for repair. There were accidents too. An LCA from *Circassia* was run down by an American LCV(P) during the second wave of the assault and a seaman who attempted to push her off went missing, while two more LCAs developed steering trouble. But the army was put ashore at very low cost. Once there, the road to Rome was open but the generals failed to push on and the opportunity was wasted.

YUGOSLAVIA – 1944

From January 1944, British forces, including motor gunboats and Royal Marines commandos, were based on the island of Vis in support of Yugoslav partisans. Four LCAs of 561 Royal Marines Flotilla arrived in April and they were fitted with canvas dodgers to operate in heavy seas. During five months they took part in nine commando raids as well as landing guns, ammunition and mules for the partisans. Again the advantages of marines in this kind of action were shown, and Lieutenant Peter Davis was awarded the Distinguished Service Cross for his action after the commandos got into difficulty.

> Lieutenant Davis who was in charge of the L.C.A.s waiting on the beach to withdraw the Commandos, organised the first five to reach the beach into a search party, armed them with Marine rifles, and, without waiting for any more Commandos, or the troop officer to arrive set off to the village where the ambush had occurred to rescue the wounded, leaving the flotilla Engineer officer in charge of craft. Lieutenant Freeman, who the enemy had left for dead when they withdrew, was evacuated to the beach by this party and probably owes his life to it.[18]

NORMANDY – JUNE 1944

Of course the invasion of Normandy, which eventually took place on 6 June 1944, was by far the biggest and most important Combined Operation of all time. The beaches were heavily defended, unlike those in North Africa and Sicily, and fitted with dangerous obstacles. For once the LCA was not expected to lead the assault. In both the British and American sectors, 'DD' or swimming tanks were to be launched first from LCTs to engage the enemy defences. In the British sector, it was also planned to land AVREs (armoured vehicles, Royal Engineers) to clear a path through the minefields and obstacles, and to send in armoured LCTs carrying self-propelled guns to engage the enemy at all stages of the action. Then the LCAs would arrive, carrying the first companies of infantry and specialist troops such as assault engineers and beach parties.

The landings had to take place during specific conditions of tide and daylight – about an hour or two after low water so that most of the beach obstacles would be exposed, and soon after dawn to give daylight to find a way through them. They were postponed from 5 June due to bad weather. The chief forecaster, Group Captain Stagg, spotted a window during the next day and General Eisenhower ordered the operation to go ahead because the consequences of any further postponement would be 'almost terrifying to contemplate'. As a result, the invasion would take place in winds of force 4 or occasionally force 5 on the Beaufort scale, more than with what a minor landing craft such as an LCA was comfortable with.

The most westerly beach was code-named Utah, and was attacked by American troops, some of them carried ashore in British landing craft from the landing ship *Empire Gauntlet*. The flotilla officers included nineteen-year-old Sub-Lieutenant Roger Lyles of Torbay, where the troops had loaded – he had watched his uncle mowing his lawn through his ship's binoculars. He and his colleagues sat up all night before the invasion playing gin rummy, before the ship anchored twelve miles offshore, and he embarked with the second wave. They arrived on the wrong beach, more than a mile south of where they had intended, but it turned out to be less well defended and the landing was successful. However, the

'Belgian barn doors', among the obstacles to be found on the Normandy beaches.

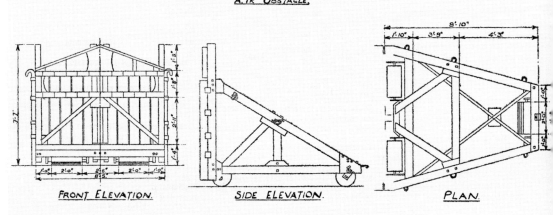

BELGIAN ELEMENTS 'C
A. Tk Obstacle.

FRONT ELEVATION.   SIDE ELEVATION.   PLAN.

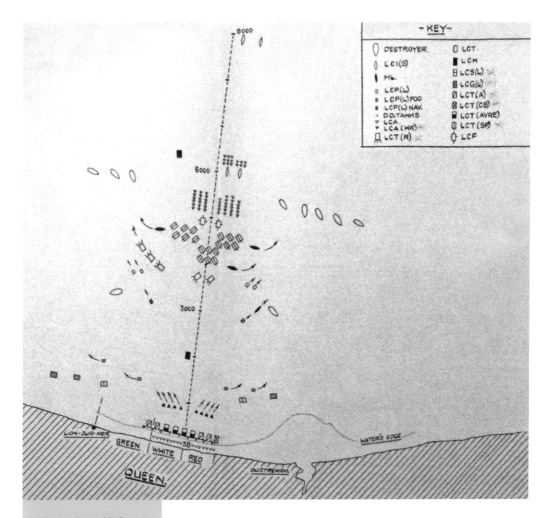

- KEY -

◊	DESTROYER.	◻	LCT
◊	LCI(S)	◼	LCM
▮	ML.	⊟	LCS(L)
▯	LCP(L)	◼	LCG(L)
◼	LCP(L) FOO	◙	LCT(A)
◼	LCP(L) NAV.	◙	LCT(CB)
ᵛ	D.D.TANKS	▮	LCT (AVRE)
ᵛ	LCA.	◕	LCT(SP)
ᵛ	LCA (HR)	✧	LCF
⎕	LCT(R)		

LION-SUR-MER
GREEN WHITE RED
QUEEN.
OUISTREHAM.
WATER'S EDGE

The landing table for Queen Beach in the Sword sector. Most of the craft types shown were not expected to land, the LCT(A)s and the DD Tanks mostly failed to do so, so the LCT(AVRE)s and the LCAs formed most of the first wave.

paratroops that had landed inshore to protect the flank were widely scattered by the bad weather, and counter attack was quite possible.

Further east near Omaha Beach, twelve British LCAs, two LCSs and four DUKWs were to land American Rangers to attack the guns that were believed to be mounted on Pointe du Hoc. On the way some of the LCAs were swamped with water. 'We found that tin hats made good bailers, but in order to give the bailers room most of the troops had to sit in an exposed position on the steel upper decks.' One of the LCSs foundered but the crew was taken off. They were guided in by a motor launch whose navigator was about to head for the wrong beach until the Rangers commander asserted himself and pointed out the error. They arrived late and the tide had risen. The DUKWs, carrying fire service ladders, could not land on the steep beaches, but the LCAs landed extending ladders and fired rockets with rope and grapnel to get a hold on the cliff above and allow the men to climb up. The point was captured, but it turned out that the guns had been removed.

Meanwhile the Second Ranger Battalion, carried in LCAs from *Prince Charles*, was intended to support the men on Pointe du Hoc. They failed to get the message and assumed that the landing had failed, so they adopted the alternative plan and landed accurately just west of the Omaha sector proper. There they were close to the landing place for the 116th Infantry, carried in six LCAs from *Empire Javelin*. One hit a submerged obstacle on the way and sank with some loss of life and the others landed in the right place, which turned out to be unfortunate. They were isolated and met a withering fire, which drove many of them back into the sea. The casualty rate may have been as high as 66 per cent.

The other assault waves to the east, carried in American LCV(P)s and also in British craft from *Empire Anvil*, were swept too far east by winds and tides and landed in great confusion. Unlike North Africa and Sicily, the enemy was ready for them and intelligence had failed to reveal the presence of a first-class German division in the area. The troops suffered heavy casualties and were pinned down for most of the day.

The British and Canadian beaches

With Utah Beach in danger of isolation and the issue in serious doubt on Omaha, everything depended on success on the three British and Canadian beaches – Gold, Juno and Sword. As in the American beaches, the swimming tanks had variable success in the rough seas. Some were launched and quickly sank, many were kept on board their LCTs and landed with them, but only after the infantry they were supposed to support. Only a few landed just before H-hour as planned. Very few of the hedgerow craft proved effective. There were several delays, particularly on Juno Beach, and the tide had risen fast in the strong northwesterly wind. The next wave, carrying the special tanks of the Royal Engineers, was too late to clear lanes to the beaches, and some reports suggest that they would not have been able to do it in time even if the weather had been perfect. As a result, the obstacles were almost intact. This left the third and fourth waves, the LCAs carrying the assault infantry. Everything now depended on about 400 leading hands and able seamen, the coxswains of the landing craft, who would have to pick their way through the obstacles and land the troops.

The bulk of the enemy forces had been sent to the Pas de Calais where the invasion was expected, and the troops had been taken off full alert because it was believed to be impossible in the bad weather. Nevertheless, they put up a strong resistance, although not on the level of Omaha Beach. But what proved worse than enemy gunfire were the obstacles laid out on the beaches. Combined Operations had produced a pamphlet that February describing the 'Element C' or 'Belgian barn doors'; the 'hedgehogs' made out of angle iron and arranged so that one point was always pointing outward; the wooden ramps and the concrete, pyramid-like tetrahedra as well as the Teller mines attached, which could destroy a small craft such as an LCA. Tank landing craft were tested against mock defences at Westward Ho in North Devon, but apart from that the crews were not given any systematic training on how to deal with them. It was assumed,

The bombardment of Le Hamel on 6 June as seen from an LCA and drawn by J C Heath.

somewhat optimistically, that the engineers would have cleared a path before the LCAs arrived in numbers.

Off Sword Beach, H T Bone was a lieutenant in the 2nd East Yorkshire Regiment and soon became aware that their role was part of a vast operation.

> In the messdecks we blacked our faces with black palmolive cream and listened to the naval orders over the loudhailer. Most of us had taken communion on Sunday, but the ship's padre had a few words to say to us. Then came the loading into craft – the swinging on davits – the boat lowering and finally, 'Away boats'.
>
> As we left the ship our bugler blew the general salute and then again we passed the HQ ship, the senior officer returning our CO's salute. Whilst this was going on, all around could be seen the rest of the convoy, with battleships and cruisers firing their big guns, and destroyers rushing round the flashes. One had been hit by something and only the up-ended part of its bows remained in view.

A famous film sequence shows Canadian troops landing from an LCA on Juno Beach in the morning of 6 June 1944.

As our flotilla swung into line behind its leader we raised our flag: a black silk square with the white rose of Yorkshire in the centre.[19]

In *Prinses Astrid*, J H Paterson was a medical officer attached to No 4 Commando.

Soon 'Lower away' sent the LCAs down in turn to bump and wrench on their davits as the swell took them. But quickly the shackles were cast off and we rode free, very free, in that sea. It was certainly rough. We waved goodbye to the *Princess Astrid* and slipped away to join the flotilla from the *Maid of Orleans*. Quite soon, thank goodness, we were allowed to stand up and look round. ...

The assault craft were together now, ahead of the bigger stuff. It reminded me of coming up to the line at the start of a sailing race. We were rolling heavily on a big swell which broke continually over us, drenching us and chilling us to the marrow.

My hands grew numb and dead and my teeth were chattering with cold and fright. The chaps in the other boats were passing round the rum, and I could hear snatches of song through the hellish din. Hutch Burt's boat went in singing *Jerusalem*. We didn't sing in our boat. My mouth was dry and I doubt if I could have produced a note. We passed round the rum, and those who were not too seasick took a good swig. The sea was well dotted with 'Bags, vomit'.[20]

Sub-Lieutenant James Leslie had a fairly typical experience in *LCA 796*. As they approached the beach they saw that the obstacles were still largely intact and just visible as the tide rose.

We decreased to as slow a speed as possible, and my coxswain, Corporal Smith, took the side-stepping craft carefully into the first line of obstacles (Element C). I swore at a teller mine which came dangerously close and involuntarily held out my hands to fend the bloody thing off, but in the last line of obstacles we were severely holed for'ard. On touching down we found that the ramp was damaged and the small steel doors between it and the well of the craft could not be opened, so the troops had to leave us over the catwalks down the sides.[21]

The 529th Flotilla from *Prince David* arrived off Juno Beach at 0825.

The tide was considerably higher than had been anticipated and the beach obstructions were partly covered with water. There were six rows of obstructions but we were able to weave our way through them. At 0840 all the craft of the 529th Flotilla were beached. There was quite a heavy swell and a strong current on our starboard quarter but due to the weaving approach it was impossible to use kedges. On the beaches there was considerable enemy fire, mostly from mortars.[22]

The coxswains of the 506th Flotilla, launched from *Duke of Wellington*, were given orders to act independently among the beach obstructions and landed their men safely. All of the LCAs of the 529th Flotilla from *Prince David* struck obstacles or were hit by mortar fire during the run in and foundered before touching down. The Canadian troops on board abandoned their packs and weapons and swam ashore to Nan White Beach in the Juno sector, ready to fight with their knives if necessary.

Enemy fire was relatively light during the run in because the defences had not been alerted due to the bad weather. Often the enemy opened fire with mortars and machine guns as soon as the craft beached.

> We landed in the proper area, but no specialised gear reached the wall. All our assault engineers were killed in action. We were still in the water when the section was cut down. … The sea was red. One lad was hit in the smoke bomb he was carrying. Another, a human torch, had the presence of mind to head back into the water. Our flame-thrower man was hit and exploded, and we couldn't even find his body.[23]

Although the LCA was armoured on its sides, its bows, stern and bottom were wooden. The Royal Marines captain in charge of the 544th Flotilla reported:

> The military were sea-sick during the run in, due to the weather. The surf on the beaches made the handling of L.C.A.s very difficult, and the craft were being thrown on to obstacles, rather than driving on to them. The stakes and hedgehogs were closely packed and there seemed to be no gaps in them on Nan White. They left no room for manoeuvre, especially when trying to unbeach. Both types were a real menace to the wooden bottoms of L.C.A.s, and as most craft casualties were due to underwater damage, it is considered that the craft mortality rate would have been much lower had there been some bottom plating in the L.C.A.s.[24]

But by chance rather than good design, the LCAs were suitable for getting through the obstacles, which were usually about fifteen feet apart while the width of an LCA was ten feet, so it was possible to weave a path through them. The forward steering position also proved an advantage here. The bigger steel-built LCTs and LCI(L)s could push their way through and were able to survive a certain amount of damage, the craft which suffered most were the wooden British-built landing craft, infantry (small) which attempted to land Royal Marines commandos to the east of Sword Beach and suffered heavy losses.

The LCA crews carried on, heeding Force J's orders that the assault was to be 'pressed home with relentless vigour, regardless of loss or difficulty'. By later morning, the landings on all the British and Canadian beaches were secure, though the tide had to rise and fall again before the engineers were able to clear the beach obstacles that evening. The landings were behind schedule and it would take longer to defeat Germany than planned.

UNBEACHING

The majority of LCAs landed their troops successfully, but found problems in retracting. Many craft found it impossible to use their kedges on the crowded beaches. The tide had risen a little more to cover the obstacles, landing craft were slightly more vulnerable in reversing out, and the beaches were increasingly congested. All five LCAs in *Glenroy's* third flight on the beach were damaged and eventually sank, although their crews were saved. For example, *LCA 279* reported:

> When unbeaching from third flight this craft was forced on to beach obstacles by a nearby L.C.T which struck a mine. Succeeded in clearing beach on one engine but water gained rapidly. Sank on forenoon of 'D' Day while alongside an L.C.T. Some stores removed. All crew safe.[25]

It was reported of one craft in the 505th Flotilla from *Isle of Thanet*:

> The troops carried in this craft all got clear of the craft and through the water but six were seen to fall while running up the beach. This boat had trouble when unbeaching, both engines becoming very overheated and once clear of the beach, it was stopped in order to effect repairs. Being unable to correct the trouble it was finally towed back to the L.S.I. by an L.C.M. There were no casualties among the crew.[26]

ELBA

Any European landing operation was likely to be an anti-climax after Normandy. On 17 June 1944, less than two weeks later, British and American craft landed French colonial troops on Elba off the coast of Italy, although the operation was largely pointless because the allied advance along the coast was almost abreast of the island and the Germans had begun to withdraw troops. Because of the danger from mines, it was decided to use nothing of deeper draught than an LST. Thirty-six LCAs, three LCA(HR)s and five LCSs were towed from Corsica by LCIs, LCTs and motor launches. The first landing to the north of the island was carried out by inflatable boats launched from American PT boats, while sixteen LCAs took the first wave in to the southwest of the island. On the way in the escorting forces had a skirmish with some German lighters which were withdrawing troops, but found no opposition on shore. The remaining twenty LCAs landed troops in the Golf di Campo, accompanied by eighteen American LCV(P)s and supported by five rocket-firing LCTs, four landing craft (gun) and the LCSs. There was heavy mining, and rocket salvos fired at the coast failed to silence the opposition for long. Two LCS and an LCA were hit by shellfire, one of the LCSs sank and the LCA burned out on the beach. They were followed by LCIs, some carrying mules which could carry ammunition over the sea wall where vehicles could not. Two LCAs were sent to take the mole at Marino di Campo, but according to Petty Officer Tom Brunton:

> Everything was dark and quiet as we entered the horseshoe-shaped harbour, but when we were halfway across to the jetty the German guns suddenly opened up – tracer poured at us and for a few seconds was only a foot above our heads. The Germans obviously thought we were closer to the harbour entrance, but then they lowered their

fire and we were hit and sinking. One shell came straight through the armoured door across the bows and the Commando sub-lieutenant caught it very severely in the face and neck. Our craft carried on through the water until we piled up on rock a few feet away from the jetty wall. Our companion craft, which was not badly damaged, came between us and the wall.

They failed to put a German flak ship out of action and at first the following wave was repulsed but the other LCA returned to pick up survivors.[27] Overall, the landings were eventually successful, but costly.

THE SOUTH OF FRANCE

The landings in southern France, code-named Dragoon, were done in far easier conditions than Normandy, with the main landings on 15 August. There were no tides, the weather was far more favourable, the beaches were better and the remaining enemy forces were demoralised. The allied ground forces consisted of three American divisions and one Free French brigade, but nine British and Canadian LSIs, some of them brought round from Normandy, participated with their LCAs. On the western flank, a Ranger landing among the islands of Levant and Port Cros off Toulon was launched from *Prins Albert*, *Prince David*, *Prince Henry*, *Prince Baudouin*, *Princess Beatrix*. *Prince Henry* had thirty-six officers and 243 men. Three of *Princess Beatrix*'s LCAs were towed into position by three fast American PT boats, while the other LCAs towed rubber dinghies towards the rocky islands and then transferred troops to these so that they could be paddled ashore. An American officer landed with what was described as an 'electric surf board'. He was supposed to guide the way in, but his light could not be seen and some of the troops were landed a little out of position.

There was no opposition on the beaches and only a little desultory fire as the craft withdrew. It was found that many of the guns on the islands were dummies. The LCAs were found to be very suitable for work on rocky coasts, and were superior to the American LCV(P)s in this respect. After the landings, the LSIs and their LCAs went to the other beaches to operate ferry services taking more troops ashore and bringing casualties and prisoners of war back. Then they returned to base to pick up more men, while some of the LCAs remained on the beaches to continue the ferry work.

On the beaches where the main landings took place, *Keren* carried thirty-nine officers, sixty-eight sergeants and 1007 men of the 48th Engineer Battalion. She launched her own ten LCAs from her davits, while nineteen American LCV(P)s came alongside and the men embarked from sally ports in the side, a procedure that worked well in calm weather. *Dunera* launched 1161 officers and men on Yellow Beach in the Alpha sector, along paths cleared through possible minefields, as the Royal Marines captain commanding the 560th LCA Flotilla reported:

> ... at 1015 hours the U.S.N. "HENRICO" signalled "Disembark all troops". At 1040 the first serial left the ship, the Flotilla being in two Divisions led by the Flotilla Officer.

The swept channels were clearly marked but very narrow, approximately 40 yards wide but with a considerable amount of debris at the water's edge.

It was decided to take the craft in Sub Divisions and orders were given to this effect. The first Sub division going in and beaching at 1050 hours. By 1103 the first serial had been landed and the craft returned to the ship.

The landings took place against slight opposition and went smoothly, except when the narrowness of the channels caused some confusion.

On the return journey to the ship after the first serial had been landed 573 L.C.A. Flotilla were encountered, also coming in to the beach to land troops, and they were informed of the conditions prevailing, despite this they did not give 560 Flotilla's last Sub Division sufficient time to clear the swept channel, consequently a collision occurred between one of their craft and L.C.A. 410 which was hoed causing the craft to take in a considerable amount of water, it was secured to another craft and brought back to the ship's side, lifted and repaired by the Maintenance Party in the space of 15 minutes.[28]

The officers and men were well trained by this time, but some of the boats were perhaps a little too experienced – it was complained that most of *Dunera*'s craft had been operating n the Mediterranean for two years and *LCA 275* had now taken part in five landings and was perhaps ready for the training flotillas. However, the LCMs were in even worse condition, and there were several complaints about them. More than 87,000 men and 12,000 vehicles had been landed after sixty hours, and that was increased to 324,000 men and 68,000 vehicles by the 25th. The ports of Marseilles and Toulon were captured and the forces headed up the Rhone valley to join the advance into Germany.

There was rather less work for the LCAs in Europe after this. As the allies advanced towards Germany they landed on the Dutch island of Walcheren, but this time they used new American amphibians, the Landing Vehicle, Tracked (LVT), instead of LCA. They found some work, however, among the Dutch islands, carrying out small-scale raids on the enemy.

Suez

Amphibious warfare languished in the Royal Navy for ten years after the war. Most combined operations officers returned to civilian life and the regulars tried to get back to the big-ship navy they had known before the war. Landing craft were laid up, often to rot slowly away. Some were kept in reserve, for example in Gareloch, off the River Clyde. The design of a new type, known initially as the LCA(2), was begun around 1950 but progress was slow. Amphibious operations revived in 1956 when the British government decided to land in Egypt after President Nasser's nationalisation of the Suez Canal. By now the LCAs were only part of an assaulting force, which also included paratroops and helicopters, but twenty were got out of Gareloch and made ready across the Firth of Clyde at Greenock, where each needed an average of three and a half days' skilled work by two men to fit new engines, petrol tanks and pipework. Even so they were in poor state after a decade of neglect and that had an impact on training. Others were found in Malta to make a total of thirty-seven available. On the voyage across the Mediterranean, the LCAs found a new role in carrying messages and documents from ship to ship, for the LSTs were not fitted with jackstays which could have been used for the transfer. Exceptionally good weather made this possible.

The beach at Port Said was very flat and this seemed to make the use of LCAs more difficult.

> A study of the beaches at Port Said indicated that an L.C.A. carrying assault waves would beach at a point about 100 yards from the water's edge in about 2ft 6ins of water. The beach itself was about 200 yards deep at this point, so that the troops would take a long time in very exposed conditions to reach the first row of houses. It was decided that L.V.T. [American landing vehicles, tracked] would be used to land the assault wave and transport them to covered positions at the back of the beach before de-bussing. As L.V.T. are slow and relatively unseaworthy compared to L.C.A it was planned to bring the L.S.T.(A) [landing ship, tank, armoured] from which the L.V.T. were launched in to a close inshore position for lowering.[29]

This allowed the men to land dryshod, although they were slow in the approach and armour of the amphibians had to be improvised – it was fortunate that there was little opposition on the beaches. The LCAs followed with the second wave and landed a minute and a half early, thirty-five rather than one hundred around the harbour. The operation was a military success but a political disaster as British and French forces had to withdraw under American pressure. As to the LCA, its day was over and the official report concluded, 'L.C.A. Mk. I should be replaced by L.C.A. Mk. II.'

Notes

Chapter 1

1 *National Army Museum Year Book*, 1, 1991, pp. 39–44.
2 L E H Maund, *Assault from the Sea*, London, 1949, p. 4.
3 National Archives, DEFE 2/782A.
4 National Archives, DEFE 2/706.
5 Admiralty Library, *Manual of Combined Operations*, 1950, CB 3181, p. 21.
6 Ibid.
7 National Archives DEFE 2/1320.

Chapter 2

1 National Archives, DEFE 2/782A.

Chapter 3

1 Website: combinedops.com
2 Admiralty Library, CB 3251, *Combined Operations Naval Basic Training*, 1950, p. 1.
3 National Archives DEFE 2/1430.
4 National Archives, DEFE 2/1429.
5 BBC, *People's War*.
6 *The Times*, 21 February 2005.
7 National Archives, ADM 1/15252.
8 Hugh Pond, *Sicily*, London, 1962, p. 78.
9 Paul Lund and Harry Ludlam, *The War of the Landing Craft*, London, 1976, p. 91.
10 Denis Whitaker and Shelagh Whitaker, *Dieppe, Tragedy to Triumph*, London, 1992, p. 239.
11 Anthony J Perrett, *The Royal Marines in Wales*, Portsmouth, 1992, p. 82.
12 National Archives, ADM 1/17685.
13 National Archives, DEFE 2/416.
14 National Archives, ADM 1/30134.

Chapter 4

1 BBC, *People's War*, Charles Bowman.
2 National Archives, DEFE 2/416.
3 Royal Institution of Naval Architects, *British Warship Design*, reprinted London, 1983, p. 35.
4 National Archives, DEFE 2/838.

Chapter 5

1 BBC, *People's War*, Charles Bowman.
2 Combined Operations Pamphlet No 37, *Infantry*, 1942, p. 5.
3 Combined Operations Pamphlet No 14(B), *Landing Craft Signal Pamphlet*, 1942.
4 National Archives DEFE 2/898.

5 Paul Lund and Harry Ludlam, *The War of the Landing Craft*, London, 1956, p. 156.
6 National Archives ADM 179/506.
7 *Bulldozer* magazine, in National Archives, DEFE 2/703.
8 National Archives, ADM 199/788A.
9 National Archives ADM 179/506.
10 *Bulldozer* magazine, in National Archives, DEFE 2/703.

Chapter 6

1 Quoted in Tim Harrison-Place, *Military Training in the British Army*, London, 2000, p. 42.
2 Combined Operations Pamphlet No 37, *Infantry*, 1942, p. 10.
3 Ibid.
4 War Office, *Infantry Section Leading*, 1938, p. 8.
5 Combined Operations Pamphlet No 37, *Infantry*, 1942, p. 7.
6 Ibid., p. 18.
7 Jonathan Bastable, *Voices from D-Day*, Newton Abbot, 2004, p. 167.
8 Combined Operations Pamphlet No 37, *Infantry*.
9 National Archives, DEFE 2/847.
10 *Bulldozer* Magazine, National Archives DEFE 2/703.
11 *Voices from D-Day*, as note 6 above, p. 189.
12 Ibid., p. 211.
13 Ibid., p. 185.
14 Ibid.
15 Ibid., p. 163.
16 Combined Operations Pamphlet No 37, *Infantry*, p. 14, National Archives, DEFE 2/1781.
17 National Archives, ADM 179/504.
18 National Archives, ADM 179/506.

Chapter 7

1 *British Warship Design*, pp. 187–90.
2 Admiralty Library, Portsmouth, Combined Operations Pamphlet No 4, *Smoke*, 1943.
3 National Archives, ADM 116/5246.
4 Ibid.
5 National Archives, ADM 179/506.
6 National Archives, ADM 179/504.
7 National Archives, DEFE 2/416.
8 National Archives, ADM 179/504.
9 National Archives, DEFE 2/1165.
10 Ibid.
11 Ibid.

Chapter 8

1 Admiralty, *The Conjunct Expeditions to Norway*, April to June 1940, 1943, pp. 72–3.

2 National Archives, ADM 199/788A.

3 Ibid.

4 John St John, *To the War with Waugh*, London, 1974, p. 41.

5 Mark Amory (ed.), *The Letters of Evelyn Waugh*, London, 1980.

6 National Archives, ADM 199/806.

7 Ibid.

8 Ibid.

9 Tony Simpson, *Operation Mercury*, London, 1981, p. 272.

10 BBC *People's War*, Charles Bowman.

11 National Archives, ADM 116/4673.

12 Denis Whitaker and Shelagh Whitaker, *Dieppe, Tragedy to Triumph*, London, 1992, p. 260.

13 National Archives, ADM 199/871.

14 Ibid.

15 Hugh Pond, *Sicily*, London, 1962, p. 72.

16 National Archives, ADM 199/858.

17 BBC People's Century.

18 National Archives, ADM 1/30134.

19 *Voices from D-Day*, op. cit., p 211.

20 Ibid., pp. 214-5.

21 *The War of the Landing Craft,* op. cit., p. 151.

22 National Archives, ADM 179/506.

23 Winston G Ramsey (ed.), *D-Day Then and Now,* vol. 2, 1995, p. 484.

24 National Archives, DEFE 2/418.

25 National archives, ADM 179/506.

26 Ibid.

27 *The War of the Landing Craft,* op. cit., pp. 219–20.

28 National Archives, ADM 199/910.

29 National Archives, ADM 1/27373.

Sources

ADMIRALTY LIBRARY, PORTSMOUTH
Combined Operations Pamphlets including:
No 4, *Smoke*, 1943
No 10, *Abbreviations and Definitions*, 1944
No 14 (A), *Minor Landing Craft*, 1943
CB 3251, *Combined Operations Naval Basic Training*, 1950

NATIONAL ARCHIVES, KEW
ADM 1/15252, Nomenclature of Ratings in Landing Craft Organisation, 1943
ADM 1/17685, Reports on technical training of naval ratings, 1942-7
ADM 1/30134, Awards to officers and other ranks of 561 LCA Flotilla, 1944-5
ADM 116/5246, Clearance by landing craft, hedgerow
DEFE 2/703-5, *Bulldozer* magazine
DEFE 2/706, Inter-Service Training and Development Centre, annual report, 1938
DEFE 2/720,Combined Operations Directory
DEFE 2/724, Combined Operations Pamphlets
DEFE 2/782A, Formation of Inter-Service Training and Development Centre, 1937-45
DEFE 2/898, Manning of landing craft, 1942
DEFE 2/1165, Modifications to LCA for use in surf
DEFE 2/1319-20, Inveraray, précis of lectures, 1945
DEFE 2/1429, Training of Stoker Drivers and Coxswains, 1943
DEFE 2/1430, Training and drafting of landing craft officers and ratings, 1942-3
DEFE 2/1781, Combined Operations Pamphlets, 1942, including:
No 6(C), *Naval Communications in Combined Operations*
No 14(B), *Landing Craft Signal Pamphlet (Other than L.C.T.)*
No 14(E), *R/T Procedure Pamphlet*
No 37, *Infantry*
WO 227/15, Assault Engineers

SHIP DESIGN
Royal Institution of Naval Architects, *British Warship Design*, reprinted London, 1983

HISTORIES OF COMBINED OPERATIONS
Amphibious Warfare Headquarters, *History of the Combined Operations Organisation 1940-1945*, London, 1956
Bernard Fergusson, *The Watery Maze*, London, 1961
L E H Maund, *Assault from the Sea*, London, 1949

MILITARY SOURCES
Tim Harrison-Place, *Military Training in the British Army*, London, 2000
War Office, *Infantry Section Leading*, 1938
William Synge, *The Story of the Green Howards, 1939-1945*, Richmond, 1952

PERSONAL ACCOUNTS
Paul Lund and Harry Ludlam, *The War of the Landing Craft*, London, 1976
Jonathan Bastable, *Voices from D-Day*, Newton Abbot, 2004
Mark Amory (ed.), *The Letters of Evelyn Waugh*, London, 1980

INDIVIDUAL OPERATIONS
Denis Whitaker and Shelagh Whitaker, *Dieppe, Tragedy to Triumph*, London, 1992
Tony Simpson, *Operation Mercury*, London, 1981,
Hugh Pond, *Sicily*, London, 1962
Winston G Ramsey (ed.), *D-Day Then and Now*, 2 vols, 1995

ACCOUNTS OF INDIVIDUAL OPERATIONS, NATIONAL ARCHIVES
Bruneval, 1942
DEFE 2/100-2

Anzio, 1943
ADM 199/873

Normandy, 1944
ADM 179/335, Training and exercise programme for Force J
ADM 179/504, Report of proceedings of Force S
ADM 179/506, Report of proceedings of Force J
ADM 199/1559, Force J, orders and memoranda
ADM 199/1561, Force S, orders and memoranda
DEFE 2/401-2, Force G orders
DEFE 2/416-7, Report by naval commander, Force G, 1944

Elba, 1944
ADM 199/2425

ADMIRALTY STAFF HISTORIES OF INDIVIDUAL OPERATIONS
All in the National Maritime Museum Library.
The Conjunct Expeditions to Norway, April-June 1940, 1943

Naval Operations in the Battle of Crete, 20th May to 1st June, 1941, 1942

The Raid on Dieppe (Naval Movements) 19th August 1942, 1946

Operation "Torch": Invasion of North Africa, November 1942 to February 1943, 1948

The Invasion of Sicily: Operation 'Husky', 1946

The Invasion of Italy: Landing at Salerno (Avalanche): (Naval Operations) 9th September 1943, 1946

SHIPS' PLANS

Very detailed plans of LCAs are to be found in the Thornycroft and Camper and Nicholson collections, National Maritime Museum, Greenwich.

SECONDARY SOURCES

Brian Lavery, *Hostilities Only*, London, 2004

Churchill's Navy, London, 2006

In Which They Served, London, 2008

James D Ladd, *By Sea, by Land, the Royal Marines, 1919-1997*, London, 1998

Anthony J Perrett, *The Royal Marines in Wales*, Portsmouth, 1992

PICTURE CREDITS

INDEX